Woiwode, Larry.
A step from death :a
memoir /
2008

OFFICIAL

37565006422934 DISCARD

LIBRARY
cent

AUG   2008

A STEP FROM DEATH

A STEP FROM DEATH

A Memoir

Larry Woiwode

COUNTERPOINT

BERKELEY

Copyright © 2008 by Larry Woiwode
All rights reserved under International and
Pan-American Copyright Conventions.

Poem on page 71 reprinted by permission of the
publishers and the Trustees of Amherst College from
The Poems of Emily Dickinson, Ralph W. Franklin, ed.,
Cambridge, Mass.: The Belknap Press of Harvard University
Press, Copyright © 1998 by the President and Fellows of
Harvard College. Copyright © 1951, 1955, 1979 by
the President and Fellows of Harvard College.

Library of Congress Cataloging-in-Publication Data
Woiwode, Larry.
A Step from death : a memoir / Larry Woiwode.
p. cm.
ISBN-13: 978-1-58243-373-8
ISBN-10: 1-58243-373-9
1. Woiwode, Larry. 2. Authors, American—
20th century—Biography. I. Title.
PS3573.O4Z473 2007   813'.54—dc22
[B]
2007033248

Cover design by Nicole Caputo
Interior design by David Bullen
Printed in the United States of America

COUNTERPOINT
2117 Fourth Street
Suite D
Berkeley, CA 94710
www.counterpointpress.com
Distributed by Publishers Group West

10 9 8 7 6 5 4 3 2 1

FOR JOSEPH

& FOR JEN

& their children

TIMOTHY & VALERIE

Contents

Time present and time past
Are both perhaps present in time future,
And time future contained in time past.

T. S. ELIOT

A man can keep his sanity and stay alive
as long as there is at least one person waiting for him.

HENRI J. M. NOUWEN

I

RECKONINGS

In the Lion's Mouth

———

So, dear son, where to begin? It could be the August morning
I stood on our front steps wondering whether to go in for a
jacket, but first let me step back as far as I can and say that what
I remember most about my beginnings, besides the voice of
my mother striding down through layers of dark to where I lay
under the wonder of the onrush of sleep, is how I felt set apart.
I didn't imagine the sensation elevated me into a special berth,
and I didn't go off to a corner of the house or school playground
to seek the isolation of a loner.

I was usually with my brother and a crowd of our friends,
but at a distance, held apart in order to observe not only what
we were up to but myself. In our age I would probably be clas-
sified as a borderline autistic or the victim of a many-lettered
attention disorder, but that doesn't cause me concern and didn't

then, or not unduly. It was my nature. I was in a trance or too busy, and it was only when my mother said I was acting groggy or unruly that I became aware of my state—in the same way I understood that my initials, when my middle name was included, spelled LAW, because she also informed me of that.

So, set apart is as close as I can come to defining the state I found myself in and still often enter. Some sort of slippage sets me there, in a displaced region that draws my attention inward. It's where I end when memory overrides the present, as now, and I search through the past in a spill of words for the moment your voice took the tone of a voice from decades ago, a phenomenon that causes a phrase of yours to adhere—another person striding down through layers of dark. Each voice affects me more as I age, especially those whose intonations I no longer hear. Death.

My work attunes me to the versatility of words. I like language that's allusive but solid enough to allow comic somersaults within its gravity, while meaning radiates from its premises to wider realms. That much is true, but my thoughts run on imagery. I *see* them. I feel I'm encountering a fog lately, however, when a recurring phrase, *Timor mortis conturbat me*, rises up. It means *the fear of death troubles* (or *disturbs* or, as somebody conversant in Latin, as I am not, suggested, *darkens*) *me*. I'm not sure fear is the right word. I watched my father fight for breath as his lungs filled with fluid and felt only rage.

I don't relish the thought of leaving your mother and you and the family on our isolated acres, not to mention the daily experiences death causes one to forgo, along with all the rest, and when I try to imagine my absence I feel as I do when I start to visualize a character for a piece of fiction—in a swirling blur of potency until he or she settles down in words.

I test all this in the displaced region. Here I examine all my acts and the words and acts of others, including every character in my fiction. Here I can travel in any direction I wish without constraint or fear of affecting others. The question at my age is, in the loss of consciousness at death (as I assume), does a trace of that region remain, as when I wake from sleep to discover I'm in bed, myself again, in the light of a new day? Or am I blank oblivion for worms? I believe I know the answer, and I do have portions of my consciousness printed in books, but that's another matter.

I did fear death when I was twenty, imprisoned in undefined stubbornness, resistant to anybody who tried to pry their way into me, while I imagined a future with strangers crowding through doors and turnstiles across the continent just to shake my hand, and *that* would show them, those inclined to tamper and pry. That was my outlook until a day when I went for coffee after a class at the university (Illinois, in Urbana) and settled into the curve of a half-moon booth of yellow-orange material called Naugahyde, and with a jolt realized that the "I" at my center might not be any more substantial than the smoke from a Lucky Strike I coughed up at the thought.

I wasn't the same after that. The booth seemed a sham of skin-adhering plastic. I believed I had a glimpse of the illusion underlying humankind—each of us only a mirror image of his or her thought. This was when existentialism, not one of its present imitations, hung like humidity in the air, so when I walked into a coffeehouse I half expected to see the moodily handsome Camus in a topcoat snubbing out with grace under pressure a stubborn Gauloise. *Living Absurd* was the text of the time.

For your sake I want to pry apart that person I guarded with such zeal, as if any intrusion could cause my psychic undoing—another form of death that I've moved in and out of enough to know it doesn't undo me for good. A year after my encounter in the half-moon booth, I was in an apartment I rented in Urbana, done with my day job, reading through *Hamlet,* as I did nearly every night, because I was planning to stage a production of the play. I would take the lead, of course.

Acting was an obsession—the way an assumed identity could affect an audience of anonymous others—and a line spoken by Hamlet, who seems a precursor of the emotion-muddled modern, shone out from the page: "There is more in heaven and earth, Horatio, than is dreamed of in your philosophy."

What more, I wondered, does he mean? I sat with my head bowed, thinking that through, when in a backwash that went so fast I felt the back of my skull disappear, I saw a panorama of branches of my family projected over separated quadrants of a huge wheel revolving around the center of my consciousness, each involved in scenes unrelated to the others yet unified in my overview, the past in the present revealing my future, and I knew it was the vision of a novel. I had failed at writing one earlier, but now I wouldn't deal with a capsized mental cripple like Beckett's *Watt,* as in my first, but five generations of a family from North Dakota.

You are the sixth generation, Joseph, at that time not yet born, and your son Timothy the seventh.

. . .

I sense an exit door at the far end of consciousness with a knob I can't turn to open it to the other side. Every detail I stumble over or move away to clear a path to the exit is a fragment of memory, and memory is a contract between the past and our instinct to shape it into a story that will cohere far into the future. A memoir should recognize that contract and dissolve the distance between us, and by that I mean not only the attentive reader, my soul's semblance, my mirror, my brother or sister, but mostly you, Joseph, my only son.

This is for you.

I don't spend days inside my head, as you know, only hours, a step from death with each tick and tock. That's the other side, and on an August morning in 2005 I stood on our front steps, wondering whether to go in for a jacket. It was 6:00 in the morning, with a fall chill raising a high wind—one of those odd August days that assault the plains after weeks of ninety-degree weather—and if an infallible warning system exists I would have walked down the sidewalk to my office and sat at this computer all day. Instead I went in for my jacket.

I work at the computer now, in pictured metaphor, as always —a patient fishing in which I follow a line of images as one would a film, hoping to draw them into resolution, the catch, *fini*. In the midst of the process thoughts rise like winter-warmed flies, drowsily clumsy but abuzz at being released, each one formed from words generated by the images I'm trying to translate.

A consolation to writing, unlike labor in the world you inhabit, is that life-threatening danger isn't at my elbow all the time as I type. That comes later, in calls after midnight, and statements of critics that distort a book so badly I sense the near miss, the saber whiz, of a death blow. My other "I" treads a tightrope where one misstep means death. I mean the horses we raise and the heavy machinery I operate to supply their forage.

We live where we do because I learned that working with my hands releases language. It always has. It's as if a sound booth is installed in some internal space, and over an intercom there I hear phrases or patches of conversation (more clearly as I'm falling asleep), and if I listen too closely, or sit at a keyboard or page, the voice clams up. But when my hands are busy at another task, especially one of earthbound or aesthetic precision— attending to a neglected corner of land, mitering pieces of trim to a tight fit—phrases and paragraphs and scrolls of pages appear behind my eyes as if inscribed on glass.

Mental preoccupation is a hazard to people who work with half-ton horses and heavy machinery, and my job that morning was to finish haying. For weeks our hay had languished in windrows—the mounded rolls that the worst of the walloping winds nevertheless carry off. I was in the midst of fixing a broken baler while your cousin Katy from Marin County and her friend, Dani, summer visitors, looked on.

The rectangular or "square" bales we produce were the only ones present until the 1970s, when round bales that look like monstrous servings of Shredded Wheat showed up. In 1978, the year we moved here, somebody stuck a pair of cowboy boots (mounted on a pair of sticks, I discovered, gullible enough to go check) in the center of a round bale beside the road, to suggest the danger. Square bales reduce the waste horses tend to make and are, besides, easy for your mother to handle when I'm away, as I must be, to negotiate that necessity, money.

I always hoped to have a horse and the hope, it seems, has overspilled. We have fourteen, plus Buddy, our penned stud. The baler you and I repaired (I'm not sure how many times), I hoped to repair once more, using parts from an even older baler in the row of machinery lined up on every rural piece of land, as if standing ready for an oncoming auction. Taking it apart grew so complicated I didn't get the better baler running until the day after Katy and her friend left.

And then not quite. I adjusted the height of the hitch that hooks to the tractor drawbar, in order to set the shaft that runs to the baler on a better line, and to compensate for that I decided to add a longer length of shaft and replace a guard missing at that joint—a job of fabrication, a circular weld you would normally do. But I was so far behind, with the windrowing done on only thirty acres of mixed grass I had planted the fall before, I felt ashamed.

I decided on a large denim jacket I usually wear over an insulated vest in winter, and with it rustling around me in the wind I ran to our 930 Case—ninety horses in harness!—which looms so large above the baler the look is of an elephant hooked to a wheelbarrow. I like the tractor's openness to the elements, with no cab, no roll bar, no sunroof—only pure weather.

The power take-off, or PTO, a geared stub at the rear of the tractor that spins at 500 rpm, was engaged as it should be to the telescoping shaft (jointed along its length to allow for turns and the ups and downs of the field) and it ran to the baler, to supply its power. Everything was greased and in shape, including the flexible joints like U-joints, with zerks at each coupling, some couplings secured by bolts, others by cotter keys, projections to watch out for.

The first warning I gave you when you started to run a tractor, the same one I got, was *Keep away from the PTO!* Even the stub shaft under the tractor seat, with its ribbed splines, can catch a sleeve or pant leg, which is why every joining has a flange of tulip-shaped metal around it, a guard. I pulled on a pair of plastic earmuffs you once used for trap shoots and target practice, insulation against tractor noise and the packer on the baler slamming home at sixty whams a minute, the baler's best speed, with the report of a shotgun. If you were here I wouldn't have had the opportunity to say to myself, *I'll replace the guard when I finish the field.* You would have said, *Now.*

I climbed the steps to the tractor seat, got it started and eased the lever to my right ahead, engaging the PTO, to check if the baler was running right. No explosion of metal.

When I was young, a writer in New York City, I remember the pity and scorn I felt when I heard that Henry Roth, the author of *Call It Sleep*—a novel of the quality of Agee's *Death in the Family*—was raising ducks in Maine. *My God*, I thought, *what has he come to!* Couldn't he find a better trade than the one I fiddled with in high school? I wasn't aware that E. B. White was living on a farm in Maine and that the studio of the Dilettante is on the Isle of Narrow Focus.

Soon after your older sister by nine years, Newlyn, was born, I read in the *New York Times* that breathing the city air was equal to smoking two packs of cigarettes a day, at a time when I was up to two myself, so we decided to move to the country and settled at so many outposts over the years that my editor William Maxwell finally said, "I hope you're there for good, Larry, because you've now filled the entire W section of my address book."

Your mother always wanted a horse and Newlyn by then was old enough to want one, not to mention my longing. I learned to write by reading and found in writers such as Tolstoy and Turgenev and Colette and others, with Wendell Berry to follow, that living on the land, especially toughing out the tillage of it, was the only way to achieve an integrated relationship with the earth, what moderns should mean when they discourse on "ecology."

I suspect not many writers know how to raise wheat (and could care less), but wheat is the source of bread and pasta, basic staples, and no writer, no matter how committed to high art, can create without food. We've raised enough wheat to feed thousands, and I don't feel any division, as I did in New York, between the writer and the person who raises animals and crops but a unity, a consolidation of body and mind in purpose.

Besides, the sedentary act of writing builds up the belly and butt and daily work keeps that at bay.

In *The Blithedale Romance*, a novel by Hawthorne, the narrator says: "Intellectual activity is incompatible with any large amount of bodily exercise. The yeoman and the scholar—the yeoman and the man of finest moral culture, though not the man of sturdiest sense and integrity—are two distinct individuals, and can never be melted or welded into one substance." I like that "finest moral culture"—a reminder of how I used to wonder whether Hawthorne would hail Hester of *The Scarlet Letter* as such a hero if Hester were his wife. You need to know, too, that the narrator of *Blithedale Romance* and his friend, Hollingsworth, are city ponces trying to set up a Robert Owen utopia outside Boston, and now are haying, the work I was involved in that August day.

Research has proved that work and exercise expand the mind, as any canny farmer knows, but the view Hawthorne set down has informed American writing for centuries—at least until recently. Annie Dillard writes, "Never, ever, get yourself into a situation where you have nothing to do but read and write," and Patti Smith says in a recent interview, "Get a job. Artists should work."

So I work. I shut down the PTO after the test of ninety horses thundering through the baler and start for the field. And see somebody running along the other side of the fence—your mother, Mom, Care, Carole—and in a few quick strides she's past the lumbering tractor and turns to point a camera at me: pictures for Katy. I ease the PTO lever forward, sending power through the baler, which appears to go up in smoke—no, the dust of hay in windrows too long—and once I'm sure everything is operating properly and see Care turn and head for the house, I settle into the task.

On your last visit, Joseph, you said, now that you're in the East, "I miss this open country." A life at the mercy of the elements isn't easy, as we learned during the worst winter in North Dakota history (bad enough to make books) in 1996–1997. But a pleasure we share without talking it thin is the exhilaration of working under the booming blue of the sky in its impact across the horizon, with rolling land rearing up in buttes, nearly pollution-free high plains country. Our place is 2,500 feet above sea level, and those who call this the Midwest should leave their studios, television or otherwise, and take a close look. You know the satisfaction of seeing machinery run without a hitch, too, especially if you've repaired it, and particularly a piece as complex and precisely timed as a baler—the reason Katy wanted to see it run.

So, Katy, the PTO shaft spins a hundred-pound flywheel and creates an inertia that is the power driving a metal packer with an elbow-like arm, over and over, into a chamber of polished steel, compacting hay with such power the entire tractor quakes. The pick-up, rows of springy feelers revolving at the front of the baler, convey the windrow into a sheet-metal mouth where tines like daggers whisk it to the left, into the chamber, barely missing the flying packer, *ka-wham*, over and over, and once the chamber is full, a pair of curved needles three feet long drive through the bale from below to a pair of knotters, and with a twist and whack two twines are tied and cut and gripped in metal fingers for the next bale.

An hour of this mechanized chatter and *ka-whamming* can have a hypnotizing effect, and this day the process is working so well, every bale tying and dropping from the chute at the back in rectangular perfection, I feel I'll never stop. Then a clog of slough hay blows a shear pin, a bolt inserted in a coupling where the flywheel and the PTO shaft connect by way of a clutch, *bang!* The pin is of brittle steel and breaks when pressure that can damage the baler builds, shutting its mechanism down. I get off, replace the pin, and start pulling the slug of hay from the baler's maw, which is so packed I have to lie over the feeder teeth and shove my head inside. I should shut off the tractor, I think; the PTO is disengaged, but what if the lever slipped and it took hold?

I look toward the house from the far end of the field. Would Care notice if that happened? I've been at this clog of hay for fifteen minutes, the tractor now shut down, everything sitting idle, and there's no sign that she's seen me.

I start up again. You and I tried to keep our fields free of rocks, Joseph, and though your sister Laurel and I picked rocks for two days before I planted the field and then cleared scores afterward, a few always surface. I get off and load them on the metal platform at the rear of the tractor, under the PTO, which spins beneath a fuel tank below the seat. Once when I stop to gather a group of smaller rocks that might shake free from the platform, I open the toolbox on the top of the tank and step up on the platform to drop them in and see that the right panel of my oversized jacket, which I haven't buttoned, is swinging close to the PTO shaft.

A fool's act. I should shut off the PTO to disengage its whirl when I dismount, especially since the repair I plan to make is of a guard—the danger I told you about, along with stories of farmers who lost overalls or a shirt, the fortunate ones, or an arm or a leg or their lives, getting entangled in one. Its spin has you so quick you can't react.

No more of that, I think, with the release of relief you feel when a truck whisks by on a busy street corner in a two-inch miss of your face while you're looking the other way.

I keep going until 10:00 and when I come to the home end of the field, a hundred yards from our buildings and corrals, I decide to stop and have a cup of coffee with Care, and then think, *Oh, one more round,* and at that second a shear pin snaps. I can't see why. The baler isn't stuffed as it was before and it's worked fine for the rest of the field.

Because the mechanism shuts down when a pin shears, the weighty flywheel ceases spinning, and only the shaft connected to the PTO rattles away. The baler settles into silence and as I throttle the tractor down to a bubbling idle, I see in the stubble below a dozen small rocks and figure the springy teeth of the pick-up flipped one into the baler. I get off and gather them up, dazed by the hours of noise, and think of how Indians revere rocks as primal material and speak to them, a view that's altered my take on rocks, which to farmers are a nuisance and scourge: *Grandfather Rocks.* I reach up for the toolbox, feel a tug at my jacket, realize I haven't shut off the PTO, and think, *My God, this is it,* and in a whirl I'm gone.

While that "I" is unconscious, let me clear up some misconceptions you might encounter. I don't seek danger, I didn't move here to embark on a Tolstoyan or religious retreat, not to mention other rumors I've read about myself, although I am a Christian and have been from the time I can remember; and we did not move to a family farm, as misinformation has it, but to an area of the state I came to love for its light and landscape when I was twelve (I grew up two hundred miles east); and it was here your mother and I found the least spoiled country once we decided to move West and spent time touring Utah, Wyoming, Colorado, New Mexico, and Montana, after living in the East and Midwest for a decade, hoping to rear you all in a pristine place. I've always enjoyed the company of working people, including writers who record the existing world to reshape or better it, rather than those so enmeshed in writing they're overwhelmed, nearly speechless, at their significance.

I was spared any memory of what happened when the shaft seized my jacket, or how it was I connected with whatever I hit, and I woke partly on the ground, in pawing spasms to get my balance, meshed in a blurring roar—the wind, the blurred and echoing noise under it my amplified groans.

My chest felt as crushed as if the field itself had fallen on me, emptying my lungs, and my right arm, from armpit to elbow, was bound so tightly by the twistings of my jacket to the PTO shaft it felt like steel. I was half on my back, hanging by the arm, suspended between present death and a future where I was free. I can't say a presence appeared to provide the help I needed, but whatever is always present took on a sparkling intensity. My eyes squeezed tears of pain but registered every detail of the tractor, stilled in the silence of a book illustration, and the ridges in the denim windings of my predicament—all at a distance I was familiar with since childhood, but now narrowed to life or death, deliverance or destruction, an entanglement that wouldn't be attended by a stadium crowd (that was the wind) but my displaced state, in a realm where the forces of silence, good and evil, contend.

Thank you, Lord, I thought, *that I'm alive.* I said it out loud. I couldn't think of another reason why a tractor of such power had killed stone dead. I was on its left side when I felt the grab but woke to see my cap and your plastic muffs behind the right tire. There was blood on the ground beside them, dripping from me, and I was sure the blazing scorch that burned with every breath meant internal injury. I spit and it came clear. As long as I wasn't coughing up blood and had control of my sphincter I would assume I wasn't dying.

Then I realized that my right arm was numb, my fingers seized with the needle-like shock of a crazy-bone bang. I looked all around, at the swelling hills and buttes on all sides, and couldn't see a farm except ours, no sign of a tractor or human being. Eight neighbors used to live in a three-mile radius and only two were left, one who planted oats here—his tractor and pull-type combine sitting idle in a field thee hundred yards off, due to overnight moisture that rendered harvesting early in the day too tough.

Against my back was the hitch that held the baler to the drawbar, the shaft binding me a foot above, and if I got my head and shoulders through the space between, I could sit on the hitch, I figured, and wait for help. When I tried this a grating pain confirmed what I already knew: broken ribs.

"Help!" I yelled, feebly, no breath. The house was out of sight, the wind so wild it cupped my cheeks when I opened my mouth. We settled here not only for the ways words arrived when I worked, but for you, Joseph, Ruth, Laurel, Newlyn—all now off on your own, Laurel leaving for college today, and I knew I never would have been caught like this, Joseph, or would be free in seconds, if you were here.

"Care!" I cried, assuming our psychic tuning would summon her. *I could as well be dead*, I said inside, speaking to her, *and don't know why I'm not, but hear me!* "Care!"

I tried calling Laurel, with a similar spiritual tuning, then again Care, craning my head in the hope of bouncing my voice off a fender. *Don't give in,* I thought, *no matter what, and you won't lose an arm or your life,* though I knew now why trapped people did give in—simply to end this.

I called for Care again and in the wind heard Buddy, our stallion, whinnying with worry and dashing back and forth in his summer pen beside the barn, sensing my distress. Carole would hear him, or Laurel, and step outside the house and hear me. I called into the wind, filling my face from the direction of the house, until I couldn't continue.

It was hard to breathe, my arm had been numb too long, and the cords in my armpit felt torn. I remembered from a first aid book that if you applied a tourniquet you had to release it over intervals to prevent damage to tissue and nerves, and knew I had to do something if I wanted to preserve the arm I wrote with. I forced my torso between the hitch and shaft, pain be damned, prying myself in place with my heels, and tugged at the wrapped-tight jacket with my free hand, wriggling the bound arm, then waving it from elbow to hand, where it dangled, and sensed feeling in my fingertips.

Whoever came, I would yell at them, "Get my pocketknife, my right pocket, and cut me loose, quick!" A swirl of dimness shocked me awake. I tried to turn the PTO but the lever that held it in gear was engaged, which meant turning the whole stalled tractor engine. I looked up at the toolbox, picturing the pliers and screwdrivers out of reach. The denim of the jacket wouldn't give a millimeter more than the half twist I seemed to gain by forcing myself between the drawbar and shaft. I couldn't raise myself enough to pull my legs through the space where I sat, worse than being ground into the dirt by a bully.

I remembered the pocketknife I meant to yell to somebody to use, but it was in my right pocket, on the opposite side of the hitch I was resting on. The jacket was so tight across my back I couldn't get my free hand half that distance. I had never felt so trapped, gripped in the teeth of a beast, a lion or worse, whose first bite would take my arm, then my head, and no matter how much I struggled and strained and yelled, nothing gave. No one came running.

I've found mice in traps, held by only a front paw, dead in an hour. Panic.

Thank you, I said again, for being alive. I had to get my left arm out of the jacket sleeve, in order to do anything else, no matter how much pain it brought, and I was learning that when

I levered my mind to a level above the pain, pain was as good as adrenaline.

The more I levered above it, though, to do what I must, the more my right arm went numb. I had to rest and breathe in pants to relieve the sensation like stalactites in my right lung and then return to reviving feeling in my hand, not as effective this time. From the force of the wind I knew nobody would hear me, and the points of pain in my chest and back registered as three broken ribs. My breath sank to moans and I felt the need for a sweet sleep swim down.

Then I heard the sound of an engine. I was on a plateau, in our surround of hills and buttes, except for a steep drop at the front pasture, where a trickling creek flows. I could see in every direction but that one, because of our buildings. The sound came from there, the frontage road past our place. The engine slowed and I saw Kim, our neighbor, who was harvesting at our place, pull up in his pickup beside the combine, climb out, and start the process of checking and greasing it, preparing to combine again. I yelled.

I watched him climb to the top of the combine to check the unloading auger, and yelled louder. He didn't raise his head or seem to hear so I gave it all I had and saw him climb down, get in his pickup, swing around, and pull off. Coming to my aid, I thought, and listened to his pickup wind up along our road, expecting him to turn in at the drive, and then saw the pickup reappear on a rise beyond our pasture and continue down the road toward his place a mile off, in a routine for him as regular as clockwork. Time for lunch.

2

A Temporary Escape

———

So, Joseph, there was no use getting my hopes up, nobody was coming, as surely as the steps of the event led to my entanglement, not to mention the wind. I had to find my own way out. I saw that as clearly as if set in print before my eyes: *This is a test.*

I had on thin leather riding gloves and I shook off the left one and lunged in that direction, hearing with my cry a rip of the jacket. But it didn't give. I worked my left hand up inside its sleeve, big enough to allow my elbow to bend, but couldn't get my arm out, once bent. And I could not draw my arm out the length of the sleeve, bound as I was.

With my fingertips I tugged at the jacket's armpit, to gain the inch I needed to get my elbow out, imagining the contortions of Houdini, and remembered a recorded voice in an odd accent saying, *If Spirit, as the texts have it, formed the worlds, then Spirit is antecedent to the physical, superior to it, and material reality must bow to it.*

So bow, I thought, and in a compression of my body I could never reproduce, my arm was out of the sleeve, free.

Still the twisted-tight jacket binding my arm would not give, and now the arm was newly numb from my contortions. But I could breathe easier and the wind was a balm over my arm and back, my shirt damp and in tatters, flapping like bannerets.

I said inside, as if speaking to Care, *I will not give up!* and in another contortion got my left hand to my right thigh and felt a protrusion, the knife, at the bottom of my pocket. I couldn't reach far enough to get my hand in the pocket so I began inching the knife up my leg from the outside—ignoring the numb swelling in my arm. The knife is of solid stainless steel, a mate to the one I gave you, with holes drilled in its handle to lighten it, so teasing it waist-ward wasn't that difficult, not counting the pain from my reach.

I finally had it to the top of the pocket, breathing hard, but couldn't get it dislodged from the inner corner. It was stuck there. I saw I was wearing different jeans from the pair I believed I had on, and in the dislocation I thought of a verse people use to suggest superhuman feats (which may be so), but in the context the writer is explaining how he has learned to be content with every up and down he encounters, whether he's full or hungry, in abundance or in need, and in conclusion says, *I can do all things through Christ who strengthens me.* I needed strength, and another line that kept revolving in me over the summer, as I swatted flies fresh from the barnyard, rose in counterpoint: *We are to the gods as flies to wanton boys; they kill us for the sport.*

The misremembered jeans and the malignity behind the line from *Lear* delivered a jolt that tripped the tip of the knife outside the pocket, shining like a star. I eased it the rest of the way out, careful not to let it slip, because I knew I couldn't reach the ground with my right arm strapped as it was, and suffered a lightheaded swim toward lights out.

I tried to open the knife's spring-loaded blade against my thigh, gripping the groove at its top with the fingernails of my inexpert left hand as I levered the handle against my leg, and had to stop to rest. I was afraid hurry would send it flying. And the previous numb swell of my trapped arm was now an arrow of pain from shoulder to wrist.

I got the blade out, grateful for its sharp point and, halfway back, a serrated edge. I punched through the denim and started sawing but had to rest, partly because as I sawed with no loosening I had to rise and twist to the right to get at the side of the jacket wound tightest. Worse pain.

I juggled the knife to get a better grip and in a slowed dimness saw it slip away, sliding down my lap. A reflex I can't explain had my thighs together so fast I wasn't aware I had stopped the knife with a swing of my numb right hand. I eased my left over to it and got a proper grip on the handle.

I had to rest again, sweating in the wind, and sensed a narrowing of my vision. *No, I can't, I will not give in,* I thought, and realized my inner speech was a form of prayer I seldom practiced, not lofty pretense. *I will not desert Care or you or Ruth or Newlyn or Laurel, no.* I redid the series of movements, beginning with the hand I knew was still agile, in order to restore feeling to my arm, because I was ready for my last attempt. I stood as well as I was able, bracing my feet for leverage, and sawed away with fervor.

I came to the collar, of double denim and leather, and couldn't cut through it, didn't have the strength, and then thought, *This is it*, and cut around the collar, not an easy route when I reached the double-thick seam at the shoulder, but in a suddenness that set me off balance I was staggering away to one side, hunched like a horror-movie monster, drooling and moaning, but free at last—free in the tearing wind.

Sensation rushed into my hand as in frostbite and I cried "Ow!" at the pain, absurd, still staggering for balance. I eased the glove off and saw my hand was blue. Pain went through it in a surge, but in spite of that and how I had to stand hunched to hold my ribs from grating, I was never so aware of how good it was to stand on legs that worked, was never so grateful for that, as I was now even in my crab-walk from the mechanical monster that gripped me. I started to drop the knife but closed it and slipped it into my pocket. Some days I forgot to carry it, and that I hadn't today seemed—

I would have wept if it weren't for bottled-up shock.

The boldest action isn't always brave; what seems bold can be a breakout of fear, though I can't say fear drove me, not even fear of death. In some internal region I knew from the beginning that I would find the way that would set me free.

I turned to the house and went sideways in my bent gait until it was in sight. No one there. Now I was angry at having to go through this, barely three hundred yards from the house, damn! And once I started staggering through the stubble the distance seemed to stretch, as if my feet were traveling backward. I made it through the white gate that leads to the yard and your mother appeared on the lawn, gliding toward me like a vision my condition called up. Then I saw a catch in her step as she took off in a run.

"Don't touch me!" I cried. "Power take-off, ribs broken. Better get to the hospital." With that frustration struck, and in the same second I sensed she was spared the shouting anger I would have used if she had discovered me bound. "Where *were* you?"

"I had to take Laurel to town." To return a set of keys to the lawyer Laurel worked for over the summer, as it turned out, before Laurel left for school—a concern that rose as she was packing. Your mother never left the place when we were in the field, but we never had an accident, and she was sure she and Laurel would be right back. Then people stopped them to talk as they attended to last-minute details.

She helped me to the entry of the house and gingerly, guided by my cries, removed the tattered shirt. I couldn't raise my right arm so she had to cut off the T-shirt beneath, and said I should see my back. She held up a mirror for me to look. The twists in the denim had dug so deep below my shoulder the flesh was laid open in raw strips, as if I'd been whipped; *by his stripes I was healed.* Laurel hovered near, pale, and I asked her the time.

"Noon," she said. So I spent two hours getting free.

"I ran to you not just because of how you were walking," your mom said, "but your face—it's gray as stone."

I was so high on adrenaline I rattled off all I could remember, how I escaped, the knife slipping, and Laurel looked appalled, growing paler, but as she and Mom guided me out the door she gave a grim smile. They helped me into the car, the most painful experience so far, now that I was free. The space the open door provided seemed undersized and both had to help lower me into the passenger seat. Your mother hopped in and pulled away from the house, and I said, "I don't think it's anything internal. Just broken ribs. *God!* Watch the bumps!"

The nearest hospital was nineteen miles, in Elgin, a trip I once made every week to do our banking. I closed my eyes and imagined a cool room inside the hospital, with a huge dose of painkiller starting to circulate. Laurel was calling ahead. But there was a catch, I thought, waking fully as it came: the doctor I trusted and expected to see had his license to practice revoked a month ago.

Three nurses met us with a wheelchair and tried to fit me into a neck brace. "For God's sake," I said, "I cut myself loose and walked in from the field! My neck's not broken!"

No hypodermic was waiting and I had to submit to the neck brace, a nurse said, before X-rays. A pair of them arranged me on the glassy slab of an X-ray table and I found that lying flat caused the worst pain yet. A technician tugged at a shoulder to position me after three pictures didn't turn out (with waits for the X-rays to be developed), and I said, "I'm not paying for the ones you didn't get right!"

About the hypo I was finally given, which was not Demerol or a similar soother, the nurse said, "This might burn a bit," and shoved a branding iron into my ass. Or so it felt.

A physician's assistant, the doctor's husband, wrote down and handed me a diagnosis that confirmed mine: "At least two broken ribs." Their curvature renders a clear read impossible in a flat X-ray, he said, and what would further knowledge gain? They hurt. The broken ends of one were pushed past each other, the PA said, "but fortunately didn't puncture a lung." From the points of pain I figured three breaks, one broken front and back, another up front.

The agony of arranging me on the X-ray table far exceeded

getting into the car, and I declined a hospital stay, which the doctor and PA gave up on, after my arguments about the neck brace and X-rays and the rest and, anyway, broken ribs aren't even taped nowadays, we learned—out of fear, it seems, of constricting the lungs and causing pneumonia. Too many lawsuits. The upper bone of my right arm, bound to the PTO shaft like a splint, wasn't broken due to the binding, but hurt like hell, as my shoulder does at this moment.

If I had reacted to the tug of the PTO, instead of going slack, I might have been smashed up worse.

Your mother noticed two lumps on the back of my head, with deep lacerations across them, when she cut off my T-shirt, and the PA said he should sew one up. He bathed both with a liquid like acid and clipped ragged pieces of scalp off one, and that was enough. The blood I had noticed on the ground was from those cuts and the metal band of the earmuffs cutting into my scalp when I hit the fender or hitch or whatever. I'm not a docile patient, if the doctor isn't one I trust, and all I wanted to do was get home and go to sleep.

But I can't sleep. I can't even lie down, and it's hard to sit, as I learn when two nurses try to help me into the car, and one says, "You're just like my dad." Resistant to interfering aid? If I was like her father I'm exactly yours, Joseph, and I know you know it's difficult to imagine the pain of broken ribs until you have a few, as you've had. A friend who went through a similar mill said, "It only hurts every time you breathe" when he visited, causing me to laugh in a complication of pain worse than a cough.

· · ·

The most comfortable position I find is in a straight-back chair, if I can settle into it myself, with no cushion, as long as it's close enough to a table to rest my elbows. But I can't sit long. I pace the house, moaning with every step, although I'm grateful to move through its rooms as a living, breathing, if crablike, being. Our house is not a rambling Victorian showpiece, as you know. It began with a central shack the homesteaders moved to the place when their first house went up in a fire, with a number of rooms added as afterthoughts, plus a three-story tower you and I attached to the south. We also cut new openings and doorways and put in insulation other than newspaper, so it has the feel of a distracted teenager in the midst of a growth spurt.

I pause in the bathroom, its interior like a cupboard viewed from the inside—every surface of cedar or redwood or oak, and find I can settle on the commode if I use the grab bars I installed for Care's mother, Grandma Peterson, during her stay with us, after she decided to remain in a wheelchair.

I've noticed how, after a death or accident, outsiders arrive and act as guides to the route one will begin to travel, and we're hardly back an hour when the daughter of the doctor whose license was revoked (I'll explain this in a bit) knocks on the door. She has a new job farther west and decided to stop on her way home to look at our horses. She and Care and Laurel stand talking on the steps where I began the day, and since she's a doctor's daughter I suspect I won't offend her if I say, as I do when I appear, "I just passed the acid test. No blood in my urine or, um, stool."

My prescription painkiller, a mild one, hydrocodone, is starting to kick in under the adrenaline. "Ow!" I cry, and then

"My God!" as I try to reach for my back, causing worse pain. "A wasp is under my shirt! It's stinging me across my back!" There is no wasp, not even a bumblebee, and a later diagnosis confirms nerve damage, a suspicion I think I saw in the expression on the doctor's daughter's face. I hobble behind the three to the edge of the front pasture, and as they go through the fence and down a steep bank to see a mare and her foal, a van pulling a trailer swings into our drive.

A piano is inside the trailer, bought by a songwriter and blues pianist who says Three Dog Night's version of "Joy to the World" is about him; *he's* Jeremiah Bullfrog. When he saw this twin to a piano he has in his basement studio, he asked if he could store it in my office as part of a grander scheme to open an arts studio in a local public school closed by consolidation. The person who sold the piano is driving the van, and the pianist, who once said to me, "I'm a paranoid schizophrenic but a dependable one," is nowhere in sight.

He's driven seven miles past our place, he tells us when he arrives, and was turning around in a drive when he saw an elderly man on a four-wheeler. "He was barely slogging along and I guess he didn't see me or hear me call, so when I ran over and caught up to him and put my hand on his shoulder to get his attention, he must have thought, *It's Satan!* You should have heard him howl!"

We store the piano against a wall in my office.

That evening Marty and Phyllis, friends who live thirty miles off, deliver a hot meal. As we're eating, or the others are while I pace and moan, Care mentions that when she and Laurel went to the lawyer's office to return the key, the lawyer looked over Laurel's shoulder and said, "Would you like to come and work for us?" and your mother, who doesn't esteem herself as highly as she should, turned to check behind her.

"No," the lawyer said to her, "I mean you."

Earlier in the summer Laurel got a recliner at a garage sale, thinking she would use it at school, then decided it would crowd her dorm suite, so I helped her carry it upstairs to her bedroom to use as a reading chair. Now she and Marty lug it back down and set it in the living room, with the idea that it will be my perfect place to rest. But when your mother and Laurel lower me into it, later that evening, tentative in every move at my protests, and start to tilt it back, I howl. The awful angle causes my broken ribs to grate.

Laurel says she's going to stay another day before she leaves for school, and gives her grim smile.

That night I can't sleep. Every way the two try to help me lie down doesn't work, or hurts too much, and sitting in an easy chair causes my body to sag so badly I can't take it. I pace and groan and finally lean against a wall and catch myself slipping to the side as I fall asleep. I can't read. I can't even think due to the concentration it takes to remain above the pain in every position I attempt—upright the best, slightly bent. And then I begin to itch all over, inside and out, from healing already beginning, I assume.

I'm sixty-three, a year older than my father when he died, in better health than I was at thirty, the only hint of age a lack of cushioning when I vault from a pickup box or off a tractor or a horse and, if a job has me kneeling or in a squat too long, a creakiness when I rise, accompanied, lately, by a groan. As I pace I think of my younger brother, Chuck, the brother you resemble, whose comic composure endears him to you, as to me—every person I think of this night is dear—and how he often says, "They say you're only as old as you feel and right now I feel ninety-eight."

I've been a creature of the night, the early morning my productive hours, so I'm not distressed at being awake—though I seem a ghost of myself in search of its end. In the midst of pacing I remember a film-like moment from five years ago, one I ignored at first, a playing out of the clearest glimpse I've had of oblivion, in pictorial terms anyway.

If I'm intuitive in my work, dreaming down metaphorical lines, I'm not a mystic or a medium, so the moment arrived with a mind-altering jolt.

It was the millennium, 2000, in early February, a month when the bottom gives out for me in sympathy with the drop it took when my mother died—January 31, 1951—at a time when I was mired in the sorrow children undergo during the month they were conceived, and its power to depress me has accelerated in the fifty years since. Unless I arm myself at the turn of the year, before this lowest ebb of winter, I feel my mind is treading water, so deep in moribund amnion I'll drown.

The jolt came the night your mother and Laurel and I were packing for Arizona in February, to see to Grandma Peterson, lately in a wheelchair by choice. We planned the trip to coincide with a conference in Wichita, where I was scheduled to give a talk and hold a workshop. I was lying in my clothes on the bed, your mother asleep, hoping to rest an hour before the sun rose, but sentences for the talk kept appearing, and then my vision shifted in a disconnected way and I saw a scene in black and white with the look of a fluttering film shot in overexposure: a rural road, the countryside smothered in snow, with a row of vans, all white, lined up along the shoulder, while with a huffing and puffing and hushed talk (sounds began to emerge) I was being trundled on my back along the line of vans, ambulances, and quick as the vision came, as if the film burned through, it was gone.

I was staring into the dark of the room, my heart beating so hard the bedsprings shook—as my heart quaked now in my late-night pacing. I'm of the mind that unsettling events are the outgrowth of experience, but this was something other, and on that morning of 2000 I tried to send the film back through the exit door to the other side of consciousness. And this night, with your mother and Laurel asleep, I leaned against a wall and thought of the person I turned to on such occasions, my editor Bill Maxwell, no longer living, and pictured him leaning back in a wooden swivel chair behind the desk in his office, saying, "To lose a mother at that age—"

It's all he says, and we sit in the resonance you feel in the air after a church bell rings in the steeple next door, and then a tear slides from a corner of his eye—the right the most prone to spill—and although he has said it to me, I know he's referring to himself, too, and his mother, who died when he was ten, and he doesn't say a word more. We attend to the resonance like tuning forks vibrating at the same frequency. He is sixty, resilient, cheerful, the only person I know who can speak with joie de vivre while tears run, but he's never been able to accept her death. "Not when it happens at the age we were," he says, and with his words the office falls away, as if our ability to hang suspended in space is the next test, since volumes of logic and psychic reconstruction—all the wisdom of the world of literature—have not set a seal on the door over the pit below, and no matter how many times I berate myself or sneer at the stupidity of a person my age (and his!) trying to explain away the effects of a decades-old death, I still feel robbed of half of my existence, the geography of womanhood, and can't rid myself of the loss any more than he.

"You learn to live with it," he says, which is the best answer I've received, and his eyes brim and run, as if he could care less about his emotion or how colleagues at the magazine call him, referring to his tears, "the waterworks."

Two days later the Elgin doctor calls. A radiologist at a Bismarck hospital that oversees the one in Elgin has located in my X-rays what he identifies as compression fractures of two vertebrae. The only way to confirm this, the doctor on the phone tells me, is a CAT scan.

"What happens if it's true, as he believes?"

"There's not really much we can do. Make sure you take plenty of calcium, and if there's any sign of osteoporosis—you smoke and are up in years—they can inject a kind of glue to help hold the vertebrae in place until they heal."

"What does a CAT scan run?"

"Let me call and ask. But offhand I would say twelve to fifteen hundred dollars."

"I'll think about it."

And since I'm a self-employed writer-rancher-lecturer without medical insurance, my thought is swift, considering there's nothing medicine can do.

Holding a phone is a feat I'm happy I can perform again.

. . .

The most comfortable place I locate is my office, in a swivel chair equipped with armrests, scooted up to a table of manuscripts, my arms on stacks of books of different heights and my head on the table between. I can sleep for an hour or two like this. I wake dripping drool, my lungs sending up an abundance of fluid, and see stacks of unfinished work all around. I've been teaching for the first time in twenty years and need to close the books on that, close out a report on an event attended by out-of-state poet laureates and local poets and professors and performers, besides finish two books.

But I can barely sort pieces of paper in my hunched stance.

The only book that holds my attention above the pain is *Early Visions*, the first volume of a biography of Coleridge by Richard Holmes. I like Holmes's wit and precision of language and his take on the dark side of Coleridge's opium addiction, which I sympathize with in my daze of hydrocodone-muted pain. It's no help to rise up and try to pace away the discomfort of sitting, so I read standing up. I move to the second volume, *Darker Reflections,* and finish the thousand pages of both in a week.

Care takes the job with the lawyer, David Crane, and it's a help to me to keep the house in order, to prepare meals for her, to pack her lunch in the morning—and not merely for the relief of a diversion. It's even a pleasure to do the dishes, since the task requires a living person, though I've hated dishes above all household chores since my brother Dan and I had to do them from the age we could manage not dropping the lot until our mother died, when it became necessary—too pitiable to see our father at them alone every night.

. . .

"You learn to live with it," returns in an echo, and I realize it was my father who taught me to step from the confines of death into work. "You learn to live with it" could as well refer to the madness of writing, which I also discussed with Maxwell; he once attempted suicide and I had an episode of disassociation that sent me to a psychiatrist.

"I'm seeing Reik again," he said—Theodor Reik, the author of *Love and Lust* (a book your mother was carrying when we met), who was his analyst for years. "He's been in retirement but agreed to see me."

"*Why?*" My concern sets his eye running, and he knocks a streak aside with a curled index finger.

"Depression," he says. "I'm also getting B-12 shots."

Nothing is as simple as it seems on its surface, and now all my projects appear to lie in a calculated disorder I designed to distract me from their disorder, no longer alert to daily life. I'm your father, a husband, and above every other occupation a writer, as Maxwell was, the reason his editing was always on spot, and I'm able to see now, as if through his eyes, that my worse ruse was to find a way to neglect my writing.

The novel it took Maxwell the longest to complete, *The Chateau,* was a finalist for the National Book Award and, according to his publisher Alfred A. Knopf (the man himself, still living), a shoo-in for the prize. But it was awarded instead to a first novel from Knopf, *The Moviegoer,* by Walker Percy. Knopf admired Maxwell's work and was so incensed he vowed never to publish Percy again, and didn't—a loyal man who allowed the Borzois immortalized in his colophon to wander through his offices. In age he took on the pear-like gravitas of Ford Madox

Ford, with Ford's yellowing mustache and glossy head, as I saw at a showing he gave, with running commentary, of slides and silent movies featuring his authors over the decades. Later he published the best of these in a Knopf book and the caption accompanying Maxwell's photo reads, "This was dear Bill Maxwell at Purchase [the Knopfs' country place] in June 1958, when the flowering crabs and the perennials behind him were in full bloom."

No other caption is so brief, direct, and personal.

Knopf was a figure of power in publishing, and few dared trifle with him, which was why I heard more than once the story of how he was having lunch in 21 when a young writer appeared and said, "Mr. Nopf, I've always wanted to meet you."

"The name is Ka-nopf," Alfred said, hitting the *K* hard.

"I'm so sorry," the young writer said. "I've only seen it in print. I didn't ka-no"—fast at least on his feet.

When I sat across from Maxwell in his office, five years had passed since *The Chateau*, a few blinks by my present measure but a spaced-out span of time then, as I went from an undergrad at Urbana who read *The Chateau* in my rented room to a resident of New York under his tutelage, and the book of his that came out the year that we listened to the overtones of that nearby bell rung was *The Old Man at the Railroad Crossing and Other Tales*. It received mostly grudging or negative reviews, and an editor at a publishing house that was soon to merge with Knopf said to me, "Well, what did Maxwell expect, with that introduction?"

It opens this way, "These twenty-nine tales were written over a period of many years, usually for an occasion, and I didn't so much write them as do my best to keep out of the way of their writing themselves. I would sit with my head bent over the typewriter waiting to see what would come out of it."

Those who know Maxwell know that his words do not imply a mindless exercise designed to celebrate an occasion but give a glimpse of the way he emptied himself to become a medium, as ancient storytellers do, employing the clairvoyant sense at the heart of his writing and editorial genius. But the tone of the introduction bothered me, once the editor weighed in, and the self-regard that governs the young, along with a kind of cannibalism—consume what you can, but only if it's in fashion—opened the first fissure of distance between us. Or so I felt, resident occupant of Maxwell's pit of depression.

"To lose a mother at that age"—the more unprepared you were, the more devastating the effect, or so Maxwell suggested.

Which is what I thought as I paced, holding my right wrist with my left hand as I would take hold of somebody I know, as I have you, Joseph, to keep you from harm.

3

Erasure

———

So how does writing go, Joseph? The Russian American novelist Vladimir Nabokov said the only way to write a novel is on
three-by-five note cards and you must always use a pencil.

Why a pencil, his interviewer wondered.

Nabokov said with Slavic emphasis, "So one can *errrase.*"

In the best writing, Joseph, erasure arrives when the first
sentence sits down right. The people in the story step in place
and I disappear. Something of my sensibility enters through the
soles of their feet, it seems, so they're allowed to mature on their
own, in another dimension. I'm merely an androgynous source
of detail, and any lack of knowledge in me about the working
of the world limits them.

I don't decide ahead who the characters are and impose pre-
ordained ideas on them. Any imposition of that kind mostly

parades your personality, or your ax-grinding ability, or your ignorance of the history of literature, when with erasure the unknown has the opportunity to arrive. So I begin each book anew. Nothing I've learned from any other (except perhaps niceties of grammar and diction) helps with the next. If a past experience appears to help, I'm probably only repeating myself.

Now, however, the act of erasure I usually reserve for fiction is, with parted ribs and the rest, my way of life, the reckoning center of a person nearly absent.

I wasn't aware how much my identity is based on health, and I was beginning to enjoy life at this end more than at the other—besides nearly every point between. I'm not angry at God or anybody else for my injuries, nor myself. I'm grateful to be alive. But on the best of days, when I'm not jerked into alertness by a jolt of new pain, I sense I'm drifting into an infant state of blank idiocy.

That, too, would be welcome, as a period to put my present situation on the shelf, if it didn't remind me of the state you endured when you were young, as I did, along with others, when the guiding word seemed *No!*—that voice striding down through darkness to say too often, "What have you *done?*"

Not so with Maxwell. He did not tell me what to do. He did not impose his ideas or writing style on me. He worked as my editor on a story I had completed and did not go over early drafts with me, sentence by sentence, as Alec Wilkinson, in *My Mentor*, says he did with him. I gave Maxwell a story I finished as well as I could at that point and in a week I knew whether the magazine was taking it or not. His work with me began then.

Once he suggested I reduce an ending before he sent the story on; another time he said the first section should be as closely written as the first paragraph, so I took it home and did that. At times he seemed amazed, perhaps appalled, when I brought in a set of "pinks" (their actual color; final galleys before page proofs) so crisscrossed with corrections it looked like spiders had gone berserk on the page. I wanted my prose to be as compact and direct as poetry as it walked the *New Yorker* columns in the blue jeans and work shirt of prose.

Once out of New York, you were the best copyeditor and proofreader I've had, Joseph, since Carmen Gomezplata. The best proofreaders experience language as the shining geography of a new world, and for many of them English is a second language, as for you, when you had to learn to use it all over again.

Two days after the accident, Care drives us thirty miles to see Marty, our rancher friend, and Phyllis. She's a nurse, the first person Care called after she saw my face and back, and they brought our meal that evening, Christians who open their wallets to us in lean times. Halfway there I realize it's too early to travel, and all I can do as they talk about spiritual matters is pace to keep above the pain.

At home, though it's dark, I sense something askew in the air, and a phone message is waiting, a woman's voice that says, "If George is there, tell him to call home." George is the doctor whose daughter appeared the day I was injured, the voice his wife's, in what I assume is a misdial. But the next morning as I sway in the kitchen, groggy from little sleep, I see George pull up in a Saab he rebuilt, and at the door he says, "I started baling last night and should finish today."

He removed my jacket from the PTO and tossed it in the box of our pickup, which he had to use to jump-start the Case 930, so he tells me—I must have left the key on. This is doctoring in a true sense, since my worry has been the hay we'll need for winter, and it isn't a neighbor or anybody from the church we attended for twenty years, but Dr. Hsu, pronounced "shoe."

His father was Chinese, his mother German, both landed aristocracy forced from their countries by reichs and revolutions.

His father was a member of the Kuomintang, one of two not executed by Mao, due to his concern for common people, but was held prisoner by Mao and then released to Chiang Kai-shek, of the opposition. Chiang forbade George's father to leave Okinawa and join his family in the United States, because of the information he held about Mao's regime. So George's mother moved the family to a low-rent neighborhood in Washington, D.C., and took a job as an embassy secretary.

They traveled to Europe on her savings and she bought George, an intellectual and sophisticate, a good suit, so he could attend embassy and debutante balls. He enjoyed the street action in their black neighborhood but was restrained from the worst by his intellect. His father mastered six European languages (besides his knowledge of Asian dialects) and learned Russian after he was sixty, because he wanted to read every Western classic in the original and had read Tolstoy and Dostoyevsky only in translation. George won a National Merit Scholarship to Haverford and majored in engineering, working in a garage that specialized in European cars for extra cash. He graduated with a record that got him into the University of Chicago's Studies in Humanities Seminar. He wanted to broaden his engineering background but after a year decided his duty as an émigré American was to enlist for Vietnam. He dismantled explosive devices there, a captain.

Back home, he left on a drive for California and was so taken by the landscape near Mobridge, South Dakota, he stopped and reveled in the Western atmosphere, the native culture, and decided *that* was where he wanted to live—an area described in *Zen and the Art of Motorcycle Maintenance,* a novel yet to appear. He persuaded a sister and brother-in-law to join him and together they bought a farm north of Mobridge, near the Standing Rock Reservation, in North Dakota, and began working the land. George loved it, every bit of it, including repairs on vehicles and equipment, but his brother-in-law didn't, and George ended up with the farm.

The 1980s were drought years, a time of forced farm foreclosures, and George, like others, began to think of a second occupation. Why not a doctor, he thought. Medicine always interested him, even then, in his thirties. He took the necessary biology and organic sciences he needed to enter med school at a local college. He graduated from the medical school in Grand Forks and opened a clinic in Elgin, served as a physician in Desert Storm and received honors, and reached the rank of colonel in the Army Reserves. Every month he attended workshops to keep him up on new practices and technology—training most physicians don't receive. He underwent hair and urine tests and other Army monitoring.

He is one of my many Dakota neighbors of distinction.

It was with you, Joseph, that I first saw his intuitive diagnostic gifts, when you suffered the head injury that robbed you of speech and were hurried to the hospital he served. As he went through a series of rapid procedures that probably preserved, if not your life, your mental integrity, before you were taken by ambulance to a hospital in Bismarck, you suddenly turned on the examining table, considerate even in unconsciousness, and vomited over its side. "Great!" he cried. "That's a good sign! He'll be OK!"

It was the only positive response we heard about you for months. When you didn't emerge from a coma for days, every other doctor was negative or pessimistic, and during your hospital stay we encountered a situation that, I suspect, led to Hsu's loss of license. A parade of specialists walked through your room, performing the same superficial tests on your inert body, or merely walked into the room and out, each adding a few hundred dollars to your bill until another doctor, an independent neurosurgeon, filed a formal complaint, and the billings disappeared.

Hsu withdrew his clinic from that hospital's oversight because of its overcharging and other such practices. The State Medical Board operates out of Bismarck, the capital, with its political and moneyed connections, and many of the doctors from the Bismarck hospital were on the board. Hsu kept up his criticisms, and referred patients elsewhere, until he was reprimanded by the board for falling behind in his written reports, a common flaw in busy physicians. When he caught up, he was charged with "inappropriate medical practice." By this the board meant, from the cases they compiled, "inadequate," but inappropriate was more damning.

They suspended his license to practice. He appeared before the board to learn why and they produced cases compiled by "an anonymous source." Every case was borderline, to such a degree Hsu said, "This is stupid." That was his real offense, along with a confident impetuousness that can be endearing; he appeared before the board without legal counsel.

He was suspended, although in twenty years of practice at a rural clinic, where you never know what will walk in, he was never, not by a patient, a family, a clinic, or a hospital, ever suspected of, much less charged with, medical malpractice. You can't buffalo thousands of patients, with their varieties of personality, over two decades if you're incompetent or inadequate in your practice. Some on the board who ruled against him had lost malpractice suits.

The board revoked his license. George took them to a local judge who ruled George should be restored but monitored for a time, in a bow to the board. The board revoked his license again. George appealed to a district court. The judge threw out most of the cases as borderline, admitting one of them *might* suggest inadequate treatment, but upheld the opinion of the first judge: restore his license, monitor him if you must. The board said no, no license for him. The judge wrote a second opinion that said, "In case you didn't understand me, let my message now be clear. Restore his license." The board decided to appeal her decision to the state Supreme Court.

George's daughter told him about my accident, and he arrived to finish my haying, a true Dakotan with me in mind.

"It looks like the medical board is trying to do away with you," I say to him.

"No matter what they do," he says, and smiles, genial as always, "they can't affect who I am. Being a doctor is what I do, not my identity. No way can they take that from me."

Timor mortis conturbat me is the refrain to each stanza of "Lament for the Makers," a poem otherwise in English. I meant to memorize it in college but kept getting caught in the Latin, and when I looked up the poem I found it was written by William Dunbar, a British poet circa 1500, and thought, *Another William in my life.* A luminous one is Maxwell, in the long backward look, but the most important is you, Joseph, or Joseph William, after we shuttled between the two until your mother decided it would be Joseph ("Never Joe," she said, "*Joseph*")—the open-throated Hebrew name for the prophetic dreamer known for wisdom, family forgiveness, and wealth.

With that in place I learned when I phoned my sister Mary Lois, the family historian, that our maternal grandmother's brother Joseph was one of the first auto-accident fatalities in North Dakota—steering wheel gone bad. I sidestepped that and said your middle name was William, and there was a pause, as if she didn't want to hear why I chose a writer and editor over my father, *our* father, who had died the winter before.

"Willie Thiel!" she cried, another brother to our grandmother, a joking child pincher in the German manner.

My mother was dead, her mother and her father were dead, and now my father and his father, too, were dead, so it was my grandmother who came with Mary to our apartment in Chicago to examine you as name bearer, I assumed. But Grandma merely laid you in her lap and smiled at you in a way that reminded me of her beauty. I saw it first in a photo album, an old snapshot of the person I pigeonholed as plain Grandma, docile but outspoken when riled, usually about religion, with a gravitational weight for making family demands.

She seemed the epitome of the stay-at-home housekeeper and then I learned from an aunt, her youngest daughter, that she used to drive a team of horses that pulled a breaking plow, guiding the plow while holding in the crook of an arm a child she was nursing (she had nine, seven sons), and when the child fell asleep she laid it in the shade of a haystack, the aunt said, and plowed on—peasant labor of the kind nobody in the family mentioned, now that our grandparents lived in town, far from the Dakotas, in a house built by my grandfather.

"Well," Grandma said, "since you already named him after my brothers, you should add the family name, too, Thiel, so people will know who this Joseph is named after."

Your mother and I looked at each other, clinging by our nails, it felt, to our fragile state—newly reunited, newly agreeable and pliable, our hippie vow of one child toppled—trying to please everybody, and nodded and revised your birth certificate to read, *Joseph William Thiel Woiwode.*

What a weight to carry through this speeded-up world!

I wake in a muddled way at 5:00 AM from a dream of my father, who's been absent from my dreams (I realize when he appears) since the day he died—or no trace of him in the dreams I recall. In a further jolt I realize I'm alone in bed, and remember Care is seeing to a grandchild of our own in a city to the south. The blank glare beyond our window, ribbed with ice, is new snow in blanketing thickness, giving off a grainy glow from the not-quite-risen sun, as if light itself is slowed by the snow's weight, returning my father as he appeared in the dream—at the height of health, his forties, with a build like a football lineman, his wavy dark hair brushed back. In my dream I did not feel my usual fear of his strength, as I did when I was young, compounded by his habit of clenching and unclenching his fists at his sides when he turned to talk to you, as if a school bully once caught him off guard and he wasn't about to let that happen again.

No, he smiles as he smiled when he wanted to conceal a surprise, and then became as bumbling as I felt when I began to write a check but couldn't find my checkbook.

The dream room was a patchwork of the last house he lived in and ours, in those alterations a dream takes to satisfy its inner logic, and he pulled a checkbook from his pocket.

"Take mine," he said. "Use it! Write the name of your bank at the bottom of the check."

I started to explain that banks printed account numbers in computer codes now, and then ran off to the room where I remembered I left my checkbook, and at that point a plumber I hired for a job (one that ended in a dispute) walked up in a banker's suit and tie—the setting shifting to the vestibule of a bank—and set down on a table separating the three of us a ten-dollar check of mine that had bounced.

In a roll under the covers, I slide into the vestibule, entering the dream at its edge to set it right, but Care's absence and the snowfall have me too alert, and I wonder whether the dream is a confirmation of the voice that entered my consciousness a year ago to say I had a decade to live, those years present in the numerals of a bad check.

I have a glimpse of the fluttering film that was my closest look at oblivion, and remember how we packed to leave for Arizona in a snowfall, and then I see my father in falling snow at the trunk of a car as he loads it for a visit to our Grandma and Grandpa Johnston's, and with a slip into that displaced address I find I'm at their farm in Minnesota, the pines laddered with layers of snow. Here I have my first sense of the outdoor scent around an inner room where petri dishes cook in the contagion and botched discards people call creativity. In this room every event is simultaneous, poised in stillness, and I can weigh one moment against another, gauging the actual worth of each, as is true of any completed book in a writer's mind, simultaneous in its scenes, regardless of their relationship to chronological

time—a godlike gaze into mini-eternity, rather than the artificial, forced imposition of step-by-step chronology. The design
you find here is a way of describing how one mind, mine,
moves—the most revealing aspect of autobiography.

For myself, I measure the meaning of every detail against
that primitive Minnesota life.

Electricity does not reach the farm until the year my grandparents move, so evening meals and reading take place under
the glow of kerosene lamps, each with its separate scent. There
is a pair of oil drums for heat, one mounted above the other,
the lower with legs of welded angle iron to hold it from the
floor, whose varnish has started to bubble; the upper for burning the gases of combustion; the entire contraption, including
a flue, backed up to a living-room wall, radiating a glow you
have to stand back from or your clothes smell of the ironing
board. Water for drinking and cooking and bathing and poul-
try and livestock—a dozen cows and a team of horses Grandpa
uses to cultivate the acreage he breaks after clearing the jack
pine—every glass or bucket of water is pumped by hand at a
hand pump from a hand-dug well. The primitive nature of the
place enhances my affection for it, in my quest to resurrect the
primal scene, although it isn't until I'm out of college that I realize I grew up in an earlier century and carry a heritage nobody
younger can know, no American will, not anymore, and here I
first sense words embedded as deep as muscles go, along with
their roots in an earlier language, an intuition of this trembling
in me as my grandmother reaches out and puts her hand over
my head.

How does she know to do this?

The history of a family begins with a woman, to condense
Cather, and the pressure of her hand produces generations

behind her, as if I'm a boy they recognize from a dream, mingling with us in a room smelling of lefse, that Norwegian potato
tortilla she rolls thin as a thumbnail, the scent of fresh bread a
bass note, and then in a crush of air she hurries to the piano and
she and my mother sing hymns in the house whose only locus is
the Minnesota woods. And in a patchy reappearance of a nearer
present, I remember hours on my knees with three generations
on my father's side, praying the rosary during Lent from the
age of eight through high school; holding a smoking censer
in church and hearing its clanking chains as the priest waves
its smoke in the direction my thoughts should tend, upward,
during the Stations of the Cross; serving during Benediction,
a miniature Mass in itself, the priest elevating a host overhead in a gold monstrance that takes on the shimmer of a star
seen through tears as he grips its base with the ends of a stole
thrown over his shoulders as though the metal will shock him
dead as he holds it on high.

My mother's younger sister is present on later trips, sitting
on the couch where she sleeps at night, and now she draws up
on its edge to recite to Dan and me

> The little toy dog is covered with dust
> Yet sturdy and staunch he stands . . .

in such a fervent voice we can't move—a schoolteacher who
married a military officer and after their son was born he abandoned her in a way not to be talked about, not in front of children, not in those days, and she and her son live on the charity
and grudging forgiveness that govern households then.

"Why, people even loaned each other their silverware when

they had guests, *for Cripes sake*," I hear my father say—the euphemism one of his favorites.

Our aunt walks past sloughs and over hills of jack pine in boots or skis in the worst of winter weather to a one-room schoolhouse where she teaches to add to the family income, and starts her day by firing up a potbellied stove. We see her return in the dark of late afternoon in her steady way across the hills behind the house, wrapped in a fur coat like a cloak over her past—a mink, somebody said, a gift from her husband, I figure—a *woman in a boyhood of trees.*

Or so I think, imagining I'm an Indian, a fantasy my brother shares, so we are Indians when our friends play Cowboys and Indians, relying on stealth and intelligence rather than the *yippee-kai-yai* of movies. We are close enough to history to see Indians in a mix of traditional and store-bought clothes walk the road that is their original trail past our grandparents' house, and I run to the road's edge when they come by, carrying two-man timber saws over a shoulder—the springing saws giving off muted musical tones—and drawknives to peel bark, along with axes and scythes, the young women with children in blankets tied to their backs, the group of them in sheepskin coats with buckskin leggings beneath or buckskin dresses trimmed with beads, wearing gray felt boots or moccasins with dyed-quill decoration.

We hold an unspoken agreement: neither side will speak, and we don't. But the summer after my mother dies, when I'm nine, I live on the farm till fall and one day look out the kitchen window and see my grandfather at the road, his jaw going with energetic talk, a past master of gab, as he says of himself, while one of the older chiefs (as I call them) in a bent-up bowler hat with a feather above the brim nods in silence.

My grandmother works the handle of the hand pump while the group watches with amusement at the way she lets water gush from the spout and splatter over the planking below until it's cold enough to suit her, and then slings the bail of her bucket behind a nib on the spout, pivoting to the side and working the handle with both hands, tall and severe looking and bone-thin, as she describes herself, though she walks with the air of royalty going to chapel, chin tucked, eyes down, carrying a shining milk bucket or a wire-handled jar wrapped in burlap out to the road, where the older men touch their tongues and the children come running in a chatter of another language, clapping.

"They aren't like a few of the farm families we know, are they," she says, "where some of the women you wonder if they heard the word 'wash.' Ish! How can they let their kids out in public so filthy dirty? You can be poor as a church mouse and still buy a bar of soap! Even water, just plenty of good water, with hard enough rubbing, will do the job!"

Her meals are better than Mom's, I think with guilt, whether it's a bacon sandwich or thick cream spooned over homemade bread and sprinkled with white sugar.

"Grandma, this is so *good!*"

"And why not? Food prepared with love is best, and when you're starved for it, why, that adds more! And I love you, you know, as you might have guessed."

I slip from her embrace, her hands callused and worn from her Norwegian need to keep active, cleaning or washing or cooking or baking or gardening or milking or butchering or canning or stirring up ingredients for homemade soap or scouring clothes on a scrub board when the washing machine won't work, and if her hands aren't busy with that she forms pleats in her dress and smooths them flat or rubs wrinkles from the tablecloth. She wants a washing machine she can plug in and sighs over models in the Sears-Roebuck catalogue (past issues stacked on the floor of the lilac-enwrapped outhouse), because her washing machine is powered by a gasoline engine with a flexible metal exhaust hose that snakes out a hole in a wall of the porch—an arrangement that leaks, she claims, causing her to lie down with a headache every Monday during the wash, while Grandpa works in the fields with his team or saws up jack pine. To start the engine under the tub with its wringers that get in the way, she has to rise up and stomp on a pedal like a motorcycle kick-start, the balky engine kicking back, bruising or scraping a shin so badly it bleeds, and the leaps can go on for ten minutes before the engine starts, while she grips the rim of the tub, so frustrated she starts weeping, a howling echo inside the tub, a terror to hear, lowering her head with its coiled braid like a crown to cry, "You damnable miserable disgusting old *brute!*"

Until she sees the procession on its route from Wolf Lake to Osage like the overflow from another century, so powerful chronology can't contain it, on their way to cut pulp for a new landowner, so she carries out a jar of lemonade and a batch of cookies, some still warm on the cookie sheet, and the children leap at her and shout and clap, causing her to laugh so hard she has to grab her mouth to hold her dentures in, while the young women smile, cheeks bunching golden and lips lifting to reveal a fleshy irregular ridge dead center.

But she's already in the house, her back to a pair of sunlit windows as she reaches out and puts her hand over my head, gripping it through my hair, and I look up and see the sunny windows obliterating her features, the light at the fringes of her braid sending up sparks. In her dim face I see my mother, and the words I intend to speak when I meet her again—a radiant version of the stumbling speech I've fallen into since she died—tremble in a tingling network over my tongue. The pressure of my grandmother's hand propels me from that all-but-wordless state toward the language that will rise from the displaced address where I presently reside.

All of which is wound around a center tight as the windings of my jacket around the PTO, Joseph, the best and perhaps the last memory of her I carry as my own, which now will evaporate, once set down.

When Dr. Hsu comes in from haying, we talk about my ribs, as friends might, since I'm careful not to draw him into giving medical advice. He comes the next weekend with his sons, sixteen and twelve, along with a friend of a son, and hauls in the bales, nearly a thousand.

By the second week the pain in my ribs starts to recede, although the one that broke overlapped heals that way, with a touchy knob sensitive to movement, and seems to catch on flesh. One night I hear bubbling inside at that spot every time I exhale. I can't sleep for the noise and in the morning I drive to the clinic and tell the nurse-practitioner I'm seeing in the absence of Dr. Hsu, "My lung is leaking! I can hear air bubbling every time I breathe."

X-rays show the overlapped rib is abrading the pleura, the sac that contains the lungs, and fluid gathers at that spot, causing the bubbling sound that keeps me awake. I can sleep in bed at last because we have a Tempurpedic mattress, but only with a pillow of its space-age substance wedged under my back.

A knotted network of muscle and nerves at my waist hurts

the worst and keeps me from bending freely, but I align a set of cabinets in the kitchen so the doors close as they should and fix and refinish a dresser stored in the basement. I do a dozen repairs around the house that I've let slide for years, and with Care working I'm not only repairman and hired hand, with chores for fourteen horses, plus a dog and cats, but cook and dishwasher and housekeeper, none of which I mind, though time takes on a different aspect. I turn around and it's gone.

When I went to New York with the hope of becoming a writer, before I met Maxwell, the idea for a first novel arrived and I sat down and began an introduction in the voice of a scholar who claims he's discovered a manuscript. The book, he says, was written by an adventurer who entered Dakota Territory before Theodore Roosevelt, when it was America's frontier, and befriended Plains Indians as he moved to the fringes, living alone, writing the story the reader is about to begin, and one day disappeared. All the scholar has is the manuscript. No trace of the writer was ever found.

4

Homestead

———

I'm of a long line at rest on home ground, as you are, Joseph—the Woiwode family has been in the state, in one branch or another, since 1881. We don't live in a cozy and sentimental Little House on the Prairie, as you know, and you would have to go East, pretty well across the Mississippi, to find a real patch of tall-grass prairie.

I spent a dozen years in central Illinois, the Prairie State, and its landscape has nothing in common with our coulees and swells and high-standing buttes. The only similarity is the sky, which here abuts against the horizon in every direction with such finality it blurs to nonexistence the few trees and sets up such an omnipresence that when we moved here from Chicago, when you were a toddler, and placed you on your back on a blanket in the yard, you startled at its expanse and then reached

54

up and drew your hand to your chest, over and over, as if drawing down floating clouds.

Naming this topography "prairie" came with settlers who had no experience of the boom of blue on green that curves off at the edge of vision like the curve of the ocean to infinity. True tall-grass prairie extends from Ohio into Minnesota, here and there crosses the border formed by the Red, the only river in the U.S. that flows north, ending in Hudson Bay, and barely continues past Jamestown, with its setting of seven hills like the hills of Rome. Once you travel a hundred miles farther, across the Missouri, you're in the West, among hills and buttes—cone-shaped, mesa-topped, and hogback—and the Missouri and Heart and Cedar River breaks.

Our average annual precip is twelve inches, counting the endless snow people imagine we have, so we're on the high plains, not prairie. Everywhere here, in the Badlands and on all but the rockiest buttes, you find the hardy short grass sought by bison—those bearded, goat-headed brutes, called buffalo, that remind me of hammer-headed patriarchs. The short grass of the plains, rich in selenium, is so nourishing ranchers drove herds of cattle all the way from Texas to feed on it over the summer, as in *Lonesome Dove*. The cattle drives weren't to Illinois, where the tall-grass prairie even then was heavily farmed.

The high plains are so arid I used to enjoy telling out-of-state unbelievers how little snow we had—in winter I mean, for those who imagine winter here is perpetual—until the record-breaking onslaught of 1996–1997, seen in *What I Think I Did*, when you and I struggled to keep the place running and our family alive.

After that, I've moderated my words.

But it would help if strangers to the state would set aside

their concept of the place as northern Alaska, and set aside "prairie," and also "Midwest"—those who never wander from the coasts and refer to the range of land from Pennsylvania to Wyoming as "the Midwest." We live far from the row-crop symmetry of that region, at the point where the real West begins, as recorded by writers such as Roosevelt and Steinbeck and Pirsig and others aware of the geophysical nature of America.

When I was in grade school and high school, we referred to the area as the Northwest, to distinguish it from the Midwest and the *Pacific* Northwest. Montana and Wyoming were once a part of the Dakota Territory, and their proximity should suggest our westerliness. Western Dakota is on Mountain Time.

But you know this, before my attempt to realign the source of most Americans' knowledge of America: television, as most of their knowledge of Europe and the Middle East and the rest of the world is television.

If I was spared a fatal twisting from the tractor to leave a last document for you, Joseph, this is it, though I'm sure you sense at times, as an only son, that you've heard plenty. A change was taking place before the PTO wrung it finer—the moment that causes me to reassess everything before and after, as if I've returned from the dead and find I'm walking the world again, Hardy's *Native Son* returned (these books are suggested readings you need not follow), though free of his stone predestinarian fate. A new person stepped from that entangling, and the "I" that was is no more.

Once I was past the stretch from thirty-five to fifty, when it seems I dispensed as much advice as others could handle (as I judge now), my inner energy started cranking up for the final bout—so little time! A wake-up came when a local provider of cowboy history said about his former work as a government employee, "You either remain a Democrat or you grow up." Or perhaps more pertinent, as Maxwell often said once he passed the age of seventy, "The perspective, Old Socks, is astonishing!"

Old Socks? I once lay on the couch in his office, for a session I'll explain, after he suggested I first take off my shoes, and not long afterward he started calling me Old Socks over the phone and in letters, and it wasn't until thirty years down the line that I was able to muster what it took to ask, "Do you call me Old Socks because of the way mine looked that day I took off my shoes in your office?"

"Goodness, no, Larry!" he said, and laughed, as he did at statements that got to his funny bone so fully it seemed they'd never let go. "I didn't even notice. It's a nickname, a term of affection! Have you been wondering about that these many years? Oh, goodness!"

I grew up a Democrat. My parents were Social Democrats of the radical Non-Partisan League stripe in a radical state coming of age. North Dakota turned twenty-one in 1910. Both went to college after the Wall Street crash, in the midst of the Dust Bowl days of *Grapes of Wrath*, when it wasn't uncommon for college students to join the Communist Party. Neither of them did. They were constrained, if for no other reason—as my father's roommate mentions in a memoir—because they had no cash for the required dues.

The liberal agenda was acute, not just jingo, after the grass-roots Non-Partisan League (composed of farmers, with Socialist underpinnings) got its slate of candidates elected to every major state office in the first year of its reign, 1917. Both sets of grandparents joined the exodus Steinbeck records, due to drought and foreclosure, one pair to Illinois, the other to Minnesota, so both sides not only read about poverty but lived it. My parents began to teach in the public schools in North Dakota at a time when teachers were revered as minor demigods, wielders of local power.

My father, out of college two years, with only a bachelor's degree, was hired as a high school principal. My mother, rearing my brother Dan and me, ran the house and money matters and taught us at home. We were reading the newspaper before I was in the first grade, which wasn't uncommon then, and by the early 1940s my father was superintendent of the high school in the village where I grew up, Sykeston.

I've heard stories of how he drove out to farms during planting or harvest and talked parents into letting a son (or daughter, in some cases) return to school rather than stay home and work. He wanted the new generation to graduate, at the minimum, from high school. They were the offspring of first- and second-generation immigrants. He struck deals with farmers, helping with the field work if a son would return to school. The person who told me this acted impressed, but I suspect my father relished the field work as much as regaining a truant. He loved the scent of turned soil, whether he was spading up our garden or piloting a tractor, and work in the outdoors gave him such pleasure he probably would have paid farmers to help in their fields, out under the sky alone.

For me, Joseph, books begin with rhythms or patterns of print, and on a January night in 2005, I was sorting through a pile of mail that came while I was away over the week, filling a temporary position at a university in the opposite corner of the state. I opened an envelope that held *The Hiawatha, 1942,* the yearbook of Sykeston High School—mimeographed sheets in a paper cover held by brass fasteners, most of the pages also bearing glossy photos glued in place by hand. It was early morning, my eyes raw from the four-hundred-mile drive, when I saw with a start my father's Palmer-perfect penmanship. Then I realized it was a mimeographed reproduction.

Swept From the Office—
    It seems rather difficult to know just what to say to you my interested reader. 1942 is a year of so many uncertainties and so many happenings of which one does not care or dare to predict the final outcome. We know we are going to face trying times in the months to come. The more education we can equip ourselves with the more will we be able to help defend democracy. Democracy depends for its strength on the enlighten-ment of the general public; totalitarianism on the ignorance of the masses. Let us choose the democratic way.
    Congratulations to the staff on their fine annual and may *You* find many hours of pleasure and enjoyment between these pages now and in the years to come.
    Sincerely,
    Everett C. Woiwode, Supt

Quite a sermon, I thought. Then I was struck by the amount he communicated in the space, and remembered how he tried out speeches on Dan and me, his voice rising into a high reg-ister, and I realized he prepared himself for these moments of purged clarity. When he wrote the paragraphs he was twenty-nine and I was six months old.

I remember you saying, Joseph, "I wish I knew your dad. I have this feeling—not that I met him, and you don't talk about him much—but I have this feeling I'd like him a lot."

You can assess that as you encounter him ahead.

The annual was mailed to me by a couple who became the legal representatives of Ivan Bern in his advanced age, the youngest of the family who homesteaded our place. Last summer at the edge of the yard I felt hardness underfoot and extracted from the sod a copper plate the size of a mailing label, with raised stamping I could read by scraping away layers of green oxide: *C. E. Bern, Burt, N. Dak.* Burt was the closest village when Charles Bern arrived from River Falls, Wisconsin, to take up his claim.

In an account of the homesteading experience written by Ivan's sister, Enid, in a county history she compiled in the 1970s, she wrote of their arrival at the railroad station in Richardton: "It was May 1, 1907, when we stepped off the train. Organized Hettinger County was fourteen days old." She expected to see fruit other than the apples common to Wisconsin because her father, on a trip to choose their homesteading site, returned with a crate of oranges from Minneapolis. Not only were there no oranges or apples, Enid noted, but not a tree in sight.

When I found the copper plate, Ivan was living in town, at the Good Samaritan Care Center—"Good Sam," as town-folk call it. I drove in and went to his room. He sat in an easy chair, a bed beside him and a few photos on a wall, with a steel filing cabinet beside a writing desk and chair.

"Oh, yes," he said, revolving the piece of copper in his fingers.

"I don't know if it has to do with the homestead, but it's Dad's. It probably came out of one of the buildings that blew away in that tornado."

He meant the tornado of 1977 that hit the farm the year before we arrived. That and the unseemly winter that followed were the reasons he and Enid, inheritors of the homestead, gave for selling to us. Ivan was in his seventies that year, Enid in her eighties, both lively and hale after completing *Our Hettinger County Heritage*, although only Enid was credited as author. She published pieces of the *Heritage*, including the portion quoted, in *North Dakota History*, a quarterly of the State Historical Society.

The tornado began near the town of Hettinger, which happens to be in Adams County, and traveled eighty miles, past Carson, in the northeasterly course tornadoes tend to take. It hit Elgin the hardest, sending a water tower to its knees, then into twisting total collapse, sweeping away houses, and driving a piece of timber through a pickup window, impaling the man inside. The fatalities included a family on a farm west of the Berns' homestead. Ivan said that when he and Enid heard the tornado approaching, they got in a corner of the basement and saw the house start to rise off its foundation, a fraction at first, and then high enough so he could see the line of trees in their shelterbelt going wild, and then it leaped the house, slamming it back on its foundation, thanks to the protective shelterbelt. It uprooted and slammed trees into buildings at the eastern edge of the farm, sending a half dozen scattering across the fields like matchsticks. A cement-and-tile silo at the back of the barn went flying.

Thirty years later, I'm still picking up nails and bits of shingle and concrete debris from the catapulting buildings—not to say the copper plate Ivan kept turning over in his fingers the year that he died.

Photos of the farm in the 1940s spilled from the front of the annual. Enid, who lived to ninety-five, began to take photographs in the 1930s, encouraged perhaps by the Works Progress Administration—a New Deal agency that funded written and photographic art, as with *Let Us Now Praise Famous Men*. Enid took photos of the farm during different seasons over the decades, as it changed and grew, and the State Historical Society gathered them in a special collection. The ones that spilled from the annual were from the wall in Ivan's room.

He worked the farm all his life and Enid helped support the place with her earnings as a high school teacher. Neither she nor Ivan married, but that wasn't uncommon then, and should not suggest a romantic duo à la Sylvia Townsend Warner. When the two of them sold the homestead of 160 acres to us—besides other acreage they had accumulated to others—they moved to Mott, twelve miles west, the seat of Hettinger County, into a modular house designed by Enid. She unveiled one of her innovations on our first visit—an insulated crawl space where a furnace hung and broadcast heat, so you could open a register in any room and draw on the general heat that warmed all the floors.

I understood her interest in warmth after our first winter in their rough-hewn house on the high plains.

It was actually their second house. The first went up in a wildfire their second year. Enid and a brother, Efford, were at the country school down the road; Charles Bern was in town with the family horse and buggy, on business. When Mrs. Bern saw the flames heading toward their place, climbing fifty feet in the air, she took Ivan to the creek in the front pasture, an act that saved them. The house and the outbuildings burned to the ground, livestock burned up inside the barn, and their horses, crowded together in a corner of the pasture not as well watered as the spot Mrs. Bern chose, had to be shot. All that remained of their belongings was the horse and buggy Charles Bern drove to town.

Plus the homestead where we now live.

The family separated and lived with homesteading friends, "until we could get our bearings," Enid wrote in her history. "Our father thought about some of the temporary shacks in the railroad camp which was breaking up. This was along the Northern Pacific tracks on the old Dobson ranch site. He made arrangements to buy one and have it moved home. It consisted of only one room, but it was quite large."

It's thirteen-by-fifteen, according to a recent measure, the central section of our house, with burn marks from a cookstove on the floorboards in one corner. The Berns added a series of additions like afterthoughts over seventy years, one of the first a sleeping porch, with windows to the north and east, installed for Ivan's sake when he was diagnosed as tubercular. He went to a sanitarium in the north of the state and came home cured, with the sleeping porch in place.

The Berns added an entry, which at first included stairs to the basement, and floored that over when they added another section, so we have two entry doors facing east. One leads to Ivan's porch, the other, the main door, into a hall where a washer and dryer once stood. You had to go through a sliding door to the left into the kitchen, through its side door to another addition, a second building joined to the first, and through an arch there

into the living room, the original railroad shack—a complicated roundabout for guests.

We put our washer and dryer in the basement the fall we
moved in, and when Grandma and Grandpa Peterson came to
visit that Christmas and were away in town, I took a chainsaw
and cut through the back of the entry into the living room.
Later I cut a door into the sleeping porch, so we could use it
as a coat room, and removed a wall behind the sink, opening
the kitchen to northern light. Upstairs, two bedrooms, plus a
bath—"The first indoor bathroom in Hettinger County," Enid
told us with pride, "installed in 1941!"—with a master bedroom
and a bath downstairs.

Tour of Little No House.

Enid was the Older Sister, the Oldest Child, the Woman of
the House, and Ivan deferred to her. She taught high school
with my father in the 1940s. The annual I held in my hands
was hers, passed on by the couple who took care of Ivan his last
years. He and Enid lived in town for a decade, and when she
died he sold the house and moved to the Good Sam. "I'm more
comfortable here," he said. The farmer who bought their house
moved it off its foundation into the country, parting it from
Enid's innovation, in a form of further homesteading.

Ivan lived at the Good Sam to the age of one hundred, always
alert when I visited, his full head of white hair neatly combed,
and showed no signs of diminishment, although I sensed an
unspoken sorrow his last year. Your mother and I attended the
celebration of his hundredth birthday, and he showed us cards
of congratulation from the governor and President Bush, the
president's on White House stationery, although Ivan was as
ardent a Democrat as Scandinavia can produce.

For the celebration he sat in a wheelchair, a jolt to me, because the winter before he made it through what his doctors called a critical phase, a bout of pneumonia, the end to many over seventy, and now this. At a lull in the party I reminded him of the first day I visited the farm and followed him around as he moved a lawn sprinkler, and how he mentioned then that he had lived on that same place for seventy years.

"Seventy-two," he corrected me.

I asked him what his goal was now that he had reached one hundred, and he looked at me with eyes magnified by the lenses he needed after years of reading by kerosene lamps—always an ardent reader—and the wavering smile I took as a show of indecision in Enid's presence rose and faded, then reappeared at the moment his mind settled, agile as ever, on chronology, "One more year."

He missed it by a month—a modest, cheerful man.

I was one of his pallbearers, the others the Berns' neighbors from decades ago, many now living in town. It was a funeral I hadn't imagined, which is to say I've imagined others, some in the overmastering mode of revenge, and it was the day before Christmas Eve. I missed the funeral parlor visitation due to my long drive to my teaching job, and tried to subdue the wallop I underwent when I walked into the church and, off in an alcove, saw Ivan's ivory face at the head of a casket.

The couple that was taking care of him, who became his personal legal representatives—the Lannans, I'll call them—handled all the arrangements, as it's said. They were members of the Lutheran Church the Berns attended and helped build—a friend said Ivan hauled rock for its walls with his father's team.

I went to the casket to avoid the appearance of evading it,

since I missed the viewing, and Mrs. Lannan, a teller I used to talk to when I visited the bank, walked up and pointed out the carved heads of wheat on the casket corners and the gold head of wheat on the silk cover raised above Ivan's face and said, "You know the meaning?"

I nodded. Wheat is the most common local crop and Ivan took part in its harvest at least sixty times, but what she meant, I knew, is that it represented a statement from one of the Gospels, in a discourse by Jesus, who says that when a grain of wheat falls to the ground, unless it dies, it produces no fruit. And I felt a further personal connection: André Gide, one of my favorite writers when I moved to New York, used the phrase for the title of his memoir, *Si le grain ne meurt*.

It was too cold to travel to the cemetery, the pastor and the Lannans decided, so the graveside rites were held in the church, and then the pallbearers followed the casket on a dolly to the hearse and then got in cars and followed the hearse to the cemetery. As we carried the casket over frozen ground, somebody slipped and I ended up holding so much weight I was sure I was going to drop my corner, and then a funeral attendant hurried up and took hold beside me until the person who slipped was back in place.

In a letter from Mr. Lannan, thanking me for taking part in the service, he said he found the annual in the filing cabinet in Ivan's room—he had given me, on the frigid day of the funeral, two framed photos of the farm from Ivan's wall. Lannan and his wife were sorting through Ivan's papers, he said in the letter, and when they came across the annual they were sure I would want it, and with it they included a copy of *Our Hettinger County Heritage*, which I had asked him for.

Some of the neighbors referred to it as "The Bern Family History," due to a number of chapters about the Bern homestead, and perhaps your mother and I were among a half dozen who knew Ivan was a collaborator—because he remembered dates and details better, Enid said, and Ivan merely nodded and added, his smile wavering, "Oh, I didn't do much."

That's a short history of my side of the history of where you grew up, Joseph. You were thirteen months old when we moved in. That fall I cut all the standing grass, even the pasture, and got it in the barn before winter hit. We set a platform of square bales outside the picture window and scattered oats across them, a feeding station for a covey of Hungarian partridge. Their offspring still hang close after three decades.

Over our first year I got uneasy at the way Enid kept asking when my next book would be out, and it's occurred to me since that she (and perhaps Ivan) expected I would be a gentleman farmer, as they became, one who looks over the landscape as he pares his nails to write.

My attraction to the land, my desire to rejuvenate and replenish it rather than laying it waste, was a heritage from my father, I see now, and the desire seemed to surprise and perhaps appall Enid. Our first decision—not to renew the lease with their renter—was, in her eyes, negative. She acted offended. But the renter used chemicals and herbicides to "bushel out," in order to increase his "cash flow," whereas our hope was to coax the land back to health and tilth by methods now known as organic. We have continued this for thirty years.

As you grew, Joseph, I realized that Enid was one of the few people who set off in you an electrical dislike. It may have been her teacherly, imperative disposition, or the way she seemed unable to give up her hold on the place, although she sold it. And perhaps your intuition, swifter and truer than my glacial process of thought, had in hand the forces at work, as surely as gravity draws my features and abdomen south.

Ivan seemed relieved to be off the farm, and I got a glimpse of why when a neighbor who knew him for sixty years said, "My God, if you could have seen how Ivan and his dad went at it! Hammer and tongs! They never got along!"

You acted up whenever we went to visit them, and weren't yourself if Enid was in the same room, especially when she happened to be sitting on the couch in her home place, which was the house we bought from her and lived in. In 1995 she turned ill at the onset of winter, as the elderly do, and settled into a bed in the Hettinger hospital. Your mother and I made several visits that weren't easy, because the only vehicle we had running was an elderly pickup with a deteriorating body and a heater that hardly worked. It was the heart of winter, late January, and Enid died in the night after one of our visits. She was ninety-five that day, a decade ago, if my math is correct. On our way home from that last visit our dilapidated pickup had a flat, an ominous sign, and I had to enlist the aid of somebody who pulled off the road to get the lug nuts off. He jumped on the wrench while I held it and the head of one twisted off.

I say "if my math is correct," because it amused my father, who taught math, to say I was no good at figures—a statement that blew mathematical ability out of my head all the way through high school and college, down to this hour.

Adults, with their store of experience and its mellowing effects, should be at least as resilient as the young. They should have flex that allows them to dive faster and deeper than youth, in order to open possibilities to a questioning or doubting or depressed young person for whom the moment, blithe enough to others, might make him or her feel forsaken. To offer that opening, without shaking a finger or sitting in judgment, is an act of mercy. And mercy is the fullest expression of love.

Too many older people harden in an outlook prescribed by their business or profession, or become dictators, trying to impose their outlook with the ham-fisted heat of a cultist beating into shape another convert.

The glory of youth is the fire of its passion.

The glory of age is its ability to bank that fire.

I consider this a sermon to myself, since I've been guilty of all I mention or wouldn't know how to name it.

The change I hope to record, to set one version of our story in place, might not go down well with those who depend on the media to define themselves. So I feel obliged to say I don't need a new car to enhance my identity, and don't have to go shopping to certify I exist, and don't watch with slavish addiction a version of the nightly news, which more and more is a fictional construct.

I don't adhere to the opinions of TV prognosticators, talking heads, or professional editorialists who repeat the sound bites of TV prognosticators and talking heads. I don't fly with a leap of faith into a political party and voice its views with the fire-breathing fervor of a fundamentalist, and I'm tired of falling in line behind a taskmaster so dependent on sound bites and talking heads the effect is of an enforcer of a cult that has no use for individual thought—on a last-ditch spree, it feels, to forge a uni-mind.

Already a form of flail defines my fatherhood, but any detail

I evade or gloss over to preserve a false sense of societal peace ("Don't rock the boat!") takes on, I've found, the glitter of significance when I'm not sure how long I'll live or how it was I stepped away from death.

So let me assure you, Joseph, before I say more, that I saw in you a son I never thought I would have and didn't deserve—one who listens. That is why, in this third version of a memoir it's taken too many years to write, I'm peeling away every layer to disclose what I hope will be helpful to you.

When you were seventeen and we were digging through clay and scoria for the foundation of a greenhouse for your mother, four feet below ground, and hauling wheelbarrows of the rough quarrying to potholes in the drive, we came up with a load of mellow soil I wasn't sure where to dump. You wheeled it to a depression at the edge of the yard, and said, "Here."

"But that's where the Berns' original homesteading shack stood," I said, "the one that burned down."

"So?" you said, and tipped the full wheelbarrow into it. I mark that as the start of our restoration to the land, when we were freed to become homesteaders here on our own. And in a dark wash far away and beyond the usual sense of loss, in a rush like your load of mellow dint sliding home, I picture you hovering, holding yourself in place above the geography of Iraq, and have to set my feet to get back to my stability.

We're in this together, wherever this reaches you.

5

Light in the Land

———

North Dakota's Statehood Centennial Poet, David Solheim,
who was commissioned to write poems over the state's centennial year, 1989, titled a recent collection *The Landscape Listens*
after the Emily Dickinson poem,

> There's a certain Slant of light,
> Winter afternoons—
> That oppresses, like the Heft
> Of Cathedral tunes—
>
> Heavenly Hurt, it gives us—
> We can find no scar,
> But internal difference,
> Where the meanings are—

None may teach it—Any—
'Tis the seal Despair—
And imperial affliction
Sent us of the Air—

When it comes, the Landscape Listens—
Shadows—hold their breath—
When it goes, 'tis like the Distance
On the look of Death—

A light like the heft of cathedral tunes inflicts heavenly hurt!
I reproduce the poem with reluctance, aware that aspiring writers will assume that this is how you punctuate poetry (along
with using archaic *'tises*), when it was Dickinson's idiosyncratic
method of suggesting pauses. Or maybe I've been asked to read
too many poems whose only punctuation is a dash.

Dickinson says that a certain slant of winter light sets us awry
at the reminder of Death's distant look, and with the arrival of
that light, even the landscape listens. I believe it does, Joseph,
registering our cries of pleasure and pain. It's neither dumb nor
numb. Sound technicians using ultra-sensitive equipment have
uncovered what they identify as human cries embedded in the
wood of old houses. Why shouldn't pliant nature receive our
outpourings equally as well?

The sounds of previous times lie dormant in the earth until a
listener releases them down the line of years. I don't know how
else to explain the wonder of a character installing himself and
talking at length, or how a landscape, a tree, even a deserted
barn can speak to a receptor, as all of the above have spoken
in my writing. The idea isn't odder than a U.S. poet laureate's
concept of the *muscular* origin of poetry, which I also believe,

in its correspondence to dance, mentioned by Robert Pinsky in *The Sounds of Poetry*. Muscular activity releases rhythmic phrasing.

Take long walks, Maxwell advised.

The language I use as a writer arrives not only from my perch on the shoulders of previous writers, using structures and techniques they explored and mastered, but from the surround of nature that over the centuries hasn't altered an iota in its makeup. All literary mystery is derailed when truth hits the tracks in a beeline toward truth's end, pressing aside precious and mystical and intellectual forethought, leaving nature unalloyed. Nature is a fundamental truth of the universe, which is why place is important to every writer.

What I noticed when we moved from Chicago (after New York) to this place was the silence. I date my work by the age you or another of the children had reached when I wrote it, and it took seven years of listening before I could say, through the sensibility of a laborer whose voice came to me in the fields: "There's a stagey thump that the virgin soil has here over unshaded ground, so unlike cultivated land, and in the surrounding painter's colors, in light undimmed by pollution, you can suffer the sensation of being on a sound stage. For a second you see the entire panorama as being constructed to contain you in its scene. Your thoughts grow in volume, as if to fill the unpopulated silence, and return in an echo; you listen for the prompter's cue."

I began to listen as I never had and some days was weaving on my feet from the "steady storm of correspondences"—to quote another poet, Roethke—streaming through me. Not that I had a language for the sounds or voices or the faintest idea of what was up. I was aware only of feeling woozy and stricken. A civilization was present before the Berns and other homesteaders arrived, as the teepee rings across our frontage road attest. I began to walk with a lighter tread but was tired by the afternoon as never before. I attributed it to the altitude, a half mile above sea level, after low-lying Chicago.

We wanted horses, which means hay. At an auction the Berns held before they left, I bought an elderly tractor and side delivery rake and tillage equipment, but no mower. An implement dealer in town said if I would supply hay for his daughter's horse, he would loan me a 1950s Allis Chalmers C with a belly mower—a five-foot sickle bar suspended from the chassis ahead of the right tire, in my view at the wheel. The mini-tractor was so maneuverable I hardly missed a square foot.

I hooked the rake to the Bern tractor and did the primary delivery of a side delivery rake, and then asked a neighbor, a dairy farmer a mile west, Julius, if he would bale it. He used a square baler, and his son, Kim, who would later farm our land on shares, drove the tractor as Julius walked behind and turned each bale so a cut edge was up, to keep mice and moisture from the twines. He did this with the flip of an ungloved hand. In the other hand he carried a pitchfork, and if the baler pick-up missed hay, he swept it up with a weaving action of the tines and laid it on the next windrow. It was careful farming of a kind I hadn't seen since I was twelve.

Our cost was a dime a bale, the going price at the time.

The best building on our place, as your mother agreed, was the barn, with a thirty-foot peak and a forty-foot-deep central section fitted with sliding doors fifteen feet high, meant to hold hay to its top. The roof sloped down to eight feet, with a wing on each side, one of which the Berns used for milking, with a milk house attached, the other with a door at each end, so you could drive a tractor through or park on concrete.

I was drawn to the shadowy interior of the barn, one window in the peak at its far end—hay-scented and cool on the hottest days—and sat in its enclosure on the stacked bales in contemplation, the only building where I felt at ease. In the others, especially the house, I kept looking over my shoulder like an intruder on the prowl, fearing the owner's return. The farm was the first property your mother and I owned, although a bank owned most of it—she thirty-four and I thirty-six, beyond the age of first mortgage holders. We always rented before, both writers in love with the outdoors.

One afternoon when I was in the barn the former renter walked in, leaning his elbows on a gate in a manner too proprietary to me, at ease here. He expected we would continue his lease, he said, and if we wanted a contract, he would be glad to sign one. A lot of locals still did business on a handshake, he said, but he preferred a contract. It put both sides at rest. He asked if what he heard we paid for the place was true. I asked what that was, and at his answer said, "About that."

"Then, frankly, you got screwed. That pencils out to over three hundred an acre."

"Not when you consider the buildings. This barn—"

"Nowadays you figure only the acreage. With the equipment you have to have these days to keep ahead, what the big fellows do is push the buildings down, then the trees. Only what you can plant you count. The land here is worth maybe two-fifty an acre, tops, and you got some real heavy soil. Your neighbor bought the pasture of Ivan's across the road for two hundred. You'll make more on cash rent. Loss falls my way."

"What kind of wheat was it you had in?"

"Prodax, a hybrid. You want that in again?"

"I think I'll be farming it myself."

"What, with that clunky old U out there?"

This was the tractor I bought at the Bern auction, the only tractor we had, as he knew.

"Yes," I said, "I might try it."

"You'll be lucky if that plug pulls three bottoms. I can get forty feet of toolbar behind my rig. I'll plant this place in a day instead of your two-bottom weeks."

He had torn down fences in a careless hurry to drive in his big rig.

"Good," I said.

"You want me to do it, then?"

"No, I meant good for you. I'll be doing it myself."

"Well, you're the boss, I guess."

Julius, who swept up our hay with balletic grace, loaned us a hayrack, and your mother and I and Newlyn, ten now, spent two weeks picking up bales and hauling them in. You were fourteen months and rode in my lap on the tractor seat, grabbing at the wheel, or rested in your mother's arms on the hayrack—an arrangement I imagined most of my life: a family working together to preserve the land.

Late one night, realizing I could follow every car and truck on the highway five miles off, my hearing reached so far I felt a backwash as my ears twitched and throbbed to open wide. I couldn't sleep for the silence. Out the bedroom window our tree rows looked frozen under a fall moon. Farther off, two miles if I could fly true as a crow, the pole light of a neighbor glowed, and in the wind rocked and sparkled like a distant star. A dove sounded its mourning notes, *ah ooo—hoo-hoo-hoooo*, and then a pack of coyotes started up their operatic prelude, yodeling from a distant hill, their chorus answered by barks and yips from far fields, and with the natural world carrying on its concourse I slipped into sleep as if listening to Mozart.

Some nights the stair steps creaked, each in sequence, as though a person were stepping downstairs. I wasn't astute enough then to listen for a residue of the Berns. Ivan chauffeured Enid out to visit every week or so, and one day he pointed to a set of gouges in the sidewalk that runs from the front steps to the pump house (struck by a tree during the tornado and knocked off kilter) and said, "The ambulance that came to take our mother to the hospital"—his lips pursed, then drew back, a smile or a grimace—"had studded tires and they got stuck and sat here and spun." He looked away to a stand of triple teepee buttes. "She never came back from that trip."

Familiarity sensitizes me to minutiae, though I'm not as sensitive as you, Joseph. You grew up and into this place, and its details form the foundation of your consciousness. The scars on the sidewalk arouse in me the sound of studded tires whirring over concrete, and when I stepped into my office today, the former pump house, I sensed a change.

I've caught a mouse, I thought, and went down the steps of the entry into the greenhouse, where I keep a trap. Mice enjoy our sprouting plants, even the habaneros I grew one winter when I hoped to have a salad garden like the Auclairs in Cather's

Shadows on the Rock. A mouse was in a trap. I delivered it to the cats. They eat them, growling, in the identical manner every time, from the skull to the tip of the tail, whole, just as copycat writers gobble up seasoned styles and modes.

When I wake these mornings, in the slow way waking occurs under the occlusion of the memories I carry, I feel an aching stab from the rib that's healing overlapped. The first minutes I'm up, it's difficult to bend at the waist, from the pain of the rib and nerve damage. Winter itself seems a memory of the change in me, the exact opposite of the winter we endured in my earlier memoir. This winter opened with a heavy snow on October 4, which didn't bode well, and snow fell again in November and after Christmas, but always with a following melt. The only danger is negotiating steely pools of see-through ice, with no wind ruffling them as they set up in their freeze.

We had a week in January like the silver silence of a writer's whiteout while getting down a patch of prose exactly right. Then came temperatures in the thirties and forties, on some days climbing above fifty, with another freeze of the pools overnight. Our driveway now is mostly mud, the fields a muddy mess when your mother and I walked them last weekend to check on the horses. Today is February 1, 2006.

And with that declaration, I realize I've made it through the January season that is usually the worst for me with hardly a hitch. I've been too busy at this.

Consistency may be the hobgoblin of small minds, as Ralph Waldo Emerson suggests, but it's also the hallmark of the ready writer, as he knew. It's the first discipline a writer has to master. *Three pages a day*, Updike vowed, a goal he felt he could reach, and has for decades, publishing nearly nine hundred pages a year. With the discipline of consistency, which is primary, the rest falls in place.

I'm preaching to myself, not you, now that I'm in a new phase of consistency. Years earlier, an internal crisis arrived on a fall day in Michigan, and I had to make a decision most writers sooner or later must make—whether my family was equal to or of greater importance than the writing. I decided greater and sat with you and Ruth and Newlyn and Laurel through injury and illness and good times and the reverse. If there was a disruption or misunderstanding in the house, I tried to settle it rather than walking off—though I have to admit I did have a knack for walking off when I was confronted in a way that stirred my emotions to such a pitch I felt my ears would steam if I tried to write. The best writer and best spouse and best parent and best friend is a confident listener.

These days, after feeding fourteen horses, a dog, and five cats, I settle in my office at the computer—after an hour of prayer and meditation to steel myself for writing, which I say not entirely in jest. And for a sense of how a workday goes, I better step back in time, for the sake of objectivity, to the morning when I was trying to rest before our trip to Arizona, when the fluttery black-and-white film appeared. What do you do after that? I reproduce what I wrote afterward:

I jerk awake and see snow clinging in lumpy calligraphy to the Chinese elms outside our window, and think, *Not the exercises, not this morning*—meaning a series of balancing and centering exercises a Dakota healer prescribed for me. I intend to go through the entire set before I start work, but usually think, as I do today, *Not this morning*—figuring I get enough exercise cutting wood or fencing or chores or whatever is necessary, depending on the season.

This morning it's packing for a trip, so I go out to my office, a squared-up version of the tornado-tilted pump house, with an extension and greenhouse you and I added, and step into a hall of bookshelves. Down the hall is a door to my office, two steps up. The long room has a low ceiling with insulation we blew in above to hold the heat. I sit at my computer and enter the sentences that were revolving in me before the vision, or whatever you want to call it, hit, and as I'm typing I feel a shudder, as if the fluttery film is about to reappear, and think, *It can't.*

And in the lag and pause I go blank.

I don't relish this trip. Too much is at sixes and sevens, although I have finished the final proofs for *What I Think I Did.* When the production editor saw them, so I heard, they caused her such upset she got on the phone to my editor in New York and said, "We can't do this!" Her printing firm dealt mostly in academic books, she said, and if any corrections were needed, *they* made them.

So the spiderwork of my handwriting (which isn't always the best) on the page proofs set her off.

"I'll clear it up," my editor told me over the phone, and when the corrections were set up for me to see, I fixed the errors that always creep in, and clarified a few passages with more spiderwork, and the same person called my editor and said, "The first was it. Not one word more!"

And when my editor called to report on the crisis, I said, "Don't I pay for the corrections I make if they exceed a certain percent of the cost of production?"

"You're right," he said. "I'll clear it up."

If you ever decide to write, Joseph, as an extension of your precision and proofreading skills, you should know that publishers no longer have in-house production staffs, as before, and workmanship has flagged. You've pointed out typos in books from the best houses. Anyway, the series of phone calls reminded me of when I finished my second novel, years late, and edited the galleys and then the page proofs in a manner that this person would surely see as excessive, but the in-house staff took it in stride, and my editor of the era, Michael, said, "Your fixes are wonderful, Larry, but why didn't you write it that way in the first place?"

"If I could have," I said, "believe me, I would." The book took ten years to finish, with two others done and out in between, but still . . . I'm never sure of the exact potential of words until I see them on a page and figure out what I meant to say, to paraphrase Flannery O'Connor. There is a barbarity in the compression a word can assume, holding a soul of multiple meanings, as with a person, in its inner space. The meanings meld into the meanings of the surrounding words, suggesting meanings I didn't mean to suggest, and a typeset page stares back with such clarity, once a book is out, I recoil at passages as I would a toad. I have to get a pencil and fix errors as I read so my ears don't burn.

The *final* finals of the memoir are off, however, and when my typing comes to a halt I begin to pack the files I'll need. To them I have to add three cartons of records for three years of back taxes (no fixing those, just pay up), plus an additional carton for the book I'm finishing, a biography that needs the support of another carton of references, reduced from twelve. I arrange them beside my office door for their fit into the Lincoln's trunk.

I again consider doing my exercises to a background of

Gregorian chants I usually choose. I know that discipline of my body put reins on my mind, as an authentic Buddhist such as Charles Johnson would affirm, and I know it's best to keep inside or *under* my body, instead of straining in a dozen directions, a trait that's caused me grief.

"Then I take an ice-cold shower and beat my back with a birch branch," I used to say, when people asked how I started my workday, until a few took me seriously.

When I'm drafting fiction, I use up too much time at my pencil sharpener. I like a razor bevel on every HB point of the brand of pencils I prefer, for the sensation of graphite gliding over the texture of recycled paper in the intimate yet resonant scratch of longhand's miniature construction—words forming sentences inside the aroma of cedar, the primitive scent I carry from Minnesota, all these sensations drawing me farther in. For essays or a talk like the one I'll give in Kansas on our way to Arizona, I settle at the keyboard, aware only of the chuckling of keys summoning sentences that appear behind my eyes.

I wade through deepening snow, sliding my boots sideways to clear a path for the next trek, and in the house arrange the boxes and suitcases Carole and Laurel have packed and set in the entry.

"Is this it?" I ask. "I hope so, because it's already too much. Do you remember I wanted to leave this morning?"

"Are *you* ready?"

"Not quite." I carry their boxes out, seeing my father in falling snow at the trunk of a 1940s Chevrolet . . .

And I'm out of the deconstructive process and back to my story.

· · ·

The owner of the winking light two miles off pulled into our drive one warm spring day—a bulky fellow with a perpetual smile, the purchaser of the Berns' pasture.

"I hear you're not leasing this year," he said. "How're you putting in crop?"

"Plow it in, I figure, with a pony drill and packer."

"That's the old way, isn't it?" He laughed, but not in a dismissive way. "I've bought up so many acres this last year my accountant says I'm a millionaire. That's on paper!"

He laughed again, and I learned his nickname was Sonny or perhaps "Sunny," due to his disposition; his speech came out in gusts of exuberance. He took a quick drag on a cigarette gripped with his thumb, cupping it in his hand, soon to quit. "I don't know how I'm going to keep up on it all, because I've got my mom's place down the road, too, and I'll have to have three rigs going to get it all planted, so I wondered if you'd be interested in running one."

I seem to step forward, as my father might, swelling with desire to be in the field.

"I know you got your writing to do, but this would only be a month and I could pay you and let you use my equipment one weekend to put in your place. What do you think?"

We both laughed.

Just as you, an only son, were at my side to help, I was an altar boy from the third grade into college, so I know how to aid whoever is running the show. The tractor I drove was hitched to a thirty-foot field cultivator, and Sunny's father followed behind, seeding. Sunny said his goal was to own land from his farm to New Leipzig, a dozen miles east, and that spring his

land ran two miles west of his place and two miles east; he had
the pasture across the road from us, his mother's place south
of Bentley, three miles off, besides scattered quarters and other
isolated pieces, and was well on the way.

He planned to keep ahead of us on the detached acreage,
which his father would seed later, but decided it was a full-
time job to keep us in parts and supplies while he attended to
another land deal or went to see his lawyer or banker, so only
two rigs ran full time. On a few fields the fall before he blew the
straw straight out of his combine, at a time when its spreader
fan wasn't working, and the cultivator I drew filled so full of
trash its teeth rose from the ground and I had to raise it with
the hydraulics and get out and disentangle straw and rolled-up
weeds from the cultivator knives. In spots where the combine
paused and poured out a pile of straw, his father scrambled out
of his tractor and lit these on fire.

One of the phrases I remember from my days as an altar
boy, when Latin was the language of worship, was translated
in the dual-language missal I used when I wasn't serving, to
read, "I have loved, O Lord, the beauty of Thy house and the
place where Thy glory dwelleth." The phrase is from a psalm,
I learned, and came to understand that a common view of the
house of glory is the earth, not the church, as I assumed when
I read it as a young server. But either works.

I jolted and swayed over the lay of the land in my tractor
seat, with the phrase revolving in my mind, and watched flights
of cranes pass overhead in a slow tilt toward their northern
breeding grounds, and shifting formations of geese, such an
onslaught of *V*s the effect was of a magician producing more
colored silks than a pair of sleeves can contain; black-and-white
lark buntings that pecked at the soil until the tractor was nearly

over them—I hit the clutch for the first few—then fluttered
past my side window to get at the succulent insects behind;
meadowlarks and horned larks and plover; pheasants tearing
off in their speedy run and flurry of wingbeats with a chuckling
cackle I could hear above the engine; killdeer acting out broken-
winged limps to lure a predator, now a tractor, from their nest,
and cottontails and jackrabbits tearing away from clumps of
grass; hawks plummeting in hits I witnessed, squeezing a rabbit
in talons and rapping its skull with a beak, beating struggling
wings to lift off with the weight, often failing, forgoing the carcass and flapping away as I drew close; a fox slinking off with a
backward smile as if to say, *I'll get you yet*; a golden eagle forgoing the slow glide of a high closing circle to dive down and carry
off the hare the hawk had dropped.

I knew we were on a major flyway but was surprised by the
gulls that followed my width of turned earth as they would a
ship's wake, setting down in their tentative bent-winged way
to feed, and not only gulls but sandpipers and godwits and
terns from the largest inland lake in the U.S. (not counting the
Great Lakes shared with Canada)—the Missouri, contained by
Garrison Dam, forming Sakakawea—and in sloughs pintails
and mallards and teals turned in watery orbits, along with an
occasional great blue heron or bittern with its neck straight up,
trying to imitate standing cattails and reeds.

It took longer than a weekend to plant our place, which
reminds me farmers are of two sorts, the overly optimistic, like
Sunny, and the stone-cold pessimists for whom nothing is right
and couldn't be worse, from the weather and lay of the land to an
insect or the grain market. The composition of our soil was, as
the former lessee put it, not only heavy (a clayey mix commonly

called gumbo) when it wasn't sandy, but so heavily fertilized over the years that the cultivator shoes hopped out of the ground, no matter how much pressure I put on the hydraulics, and jittered over the crusted surface.

That was why I wanted to plow, and why we hoped to renew the health of the soil by farming practices wholly organic.

Over my stints as a hired hand in North Dakota and Illinois I drove open tractors and couldn't get over the insulated feel of a cab, how it contained the roar of the enormous diesel engine, besides the irritation of trying to see past a metal brace or window frame to the ground. One evening, late, when I was returning Sunny's equipment by the overland route of a ragged section line, navigating by headlights that didn't reach far enough ahead, I had a sudden sense inside the wallowing strum of the tractor, with its lighted dials below, of piloting a lumbering aircraft, a 747, my oasis of lighted ground like a city below, and realized that for all the field work I had been doing and all the fowl and wildlife I had *seen*, I never had a sense of knowing the land by its scent and tilth and was, to tell the truth, out of touch with it. So were all who piloted tractors of this size, in the era of soundproofing and in-cab stereos and computers and television sets, guiding a monster down a mile stretch of land as they left a forty-foot swath of raw soil in their wake.

It took several weekends and a Monday to till and plant our place, partly due to a breakdown. It was early evening and a hitch on one of the gangs of teeth on the cultivator broke. It was the fault of my impatience; I got the tractor stuck and started to back up, which you shouldn't do with a cultivator, especially one in several sections, but I was in a hurry to plant our place.

I heard the snap of steel and got out and saw it would take a new part to repair it, if not a weld of pieces to receive the part. There was nothing I could do but shut the tractor down and walk home.

I was on a rise to the south of the house and as I made my way in the toiling steps it takes to navigate turned earth I realized I was breathing the scent that first drew me to work the land. *Soil.* Earth itself. How happy I was to think we would return it to its original state! To my left a sunset of yellow and green, colors rarely seen in the Midwest, spread altering shapes along an orange crest above the horizon. I slowed as I neared our place at the appearance of the lawn.

Newlyn had been mowing it, as I saw when I was working the field, a chore she enjoyed, but it wasn't only that. In the light the lawn looked emerald and with my first step onto it, I sensed it as a membranous texture giving way. I could see every blade of grass and its colored shadow, as if the entire lawn, like hair, had been combed. Shafts of light through the tree rows set yellow-gold patches over its surface, and the trees had the appearance of sculptures glowing from within. Not one leaf twitched on any, as if to assert the timelessness the moment had assumed. I had stepped into Eden, and felt moisture falling in the evening air all around and over the house where the first lights came on, revealing your mother at work with you and Newlyn at her side.

6

Sonship

I was not a dependable son, no stalwart behind my father. It was too easy for me to find flaws in him, and this blurred my ability, I believe, to be transparent with you, Joseph, as the best fathers are. I imagined judgment or wounding on the way and kept inner tracts undisclosed—withdrawn and secretive rather than a guide to you and your needs.

I read an essay in the 1970s by John Leonard, an editor at the *Times Book Review* who later became a cultural commentator at the *Times,* and the gist of his message was the lack of depth about fathers in American writing. What we need, he said in essence, is a prodigious new novel on fatherhood. I was struck by this but not wholly sure what he meant. I dedicated *Beyond the Bedroom Wall* to my father and believed (in the way writers refer to their books) that its center was a father with other fathers offering variations on fatherhood.

I won't paw the ashes of false modesty, the *Aw-shucks!* attitude of people with such huge self-esteem they can't stand assessment or praise, because neither is right or sufficient. My clearer litmus is my father. He was visiting at one of our temporary outposts when I showed him an early version of a chapter of *Beyond the Bedroom Wall* I had sold as a story. He read it through, and without allowing him a pause to let it sink in, I said, as writers will, "What do you think?"

"It's well written, a wonderful story, especially this next-to-last scene, then the end. Your endings are always good. But I'm not sure what to think about the father in it. I'm not sure I'd want to meet the guy!"

I tried to shove aside his misgivings, insisting that the father was the reason for the story, its pivot. "Yes, but . . ." But later I saw in *Bedroom Wall* a sense of amusement, an added spin, in my depictions of Martin, the central Neumiller father, who bore some resemblance to mine, yes.

After the novel appeared I was invited to meet with a panel of psychiatrists for "The Mellon Series on Mentally Healthy Characters in American Fiction" (and the opposite, as one might suspect) and the consensus of the group, especially a persnickety and abusive white-haired professor emerita, was that Martin was not bright, was gullible and self-serving, whereas Alpha, his wife, was his brilliant and selfless and, one assumes, "mentally healthy" foil. I was offended. Martin is ingenuous, as seen in the novel, not a dunderhead rooting at his mother, as the professor emerita implied.

Writing about the relationship of a son to a father—in fiction,

I mean—felt strained, if not insuperable, then. I found few examples of sonship in American fiction, as John Leonard noted, when in the novels of Tolstoy and Turgenev and Dostoyevsky, for instance, fatherhood is seen from multiple perspectives, with no set viewpoint. What I notice about most fathers in American fiction, besides their role as dunces, is the list of complaints against them, so common they're clichés, if not railing against fatherhood itself.

This is especially true in recent years.

John Updike's *Pigeon Feathers* and *The Centaur* are exceptions, but as his work moved on he seemed to mistrust fatherhood with a growing force, or anyway his version of it, while Paternalism put on a suit of horns and a tail, plus the pitchfork, and made his rounds of the university circuit.

Injustices have occurred in the name of paternalism, surely, including a tendency to imprison, whether a woman or a child or a culture or an entire country, as in colonialism, but paternalism was not then or now the evil responsible for every dislocation in humankind. Lack of love hits closer and that lack appears on every side of the intellectual and political spectrum, anytime a dictatorial tone enters an explanation or discussion.

The prevailing mistrust of a patriarch soon translated to mean "father" and invaded my work, I admit, although I was a father myself by then, and the invasion seems one I welcomed. Down with Dad!

I admired him for his spiritual fortitude after my mother's death but couldn't express what I felt and what I was sure other sons felt, too. I tended to depict fathers with condescension or irony or got bogged down trying to improve my descriptions of them. The words wouldn't spring from their sentences with the speed of light, as it feels when I'm tripped into the dimension of creative delirium and glimpse a wink of eternity, as in "the seal's wide spindrift gaze toward paradise" in the wonderful conclusion to a Hart Crane poem.

I felt I was on a paternal path in my relationship with Maxwell, a give-and-take of mutual regard, and saw in him the figure of a father. When I tried to explain this to your mother, early on, I said, "I think I see him as my literary father." Her eyes widened, revealing the darker complexity in their depths, as if to say, *Am I hearing you right?*

Her love for my father was unalloyed and enduring.

A view I held, surely romantic, was that since Maxwell and I lost our mothers we were searchers for an assurance always absent—the edge to our writing. Did that cause unreason in us about our fathers, insensitivity to their trials as adults? We both wrote of our need for our fathers in the aftermath of death and our wills to survive. We both spoke of our fathers with affection. He admired mine.

But Maxwell's temperament, refined and literary, was on a different level. I was driven by emotion and doubt, he by reconsideration of loss. In his *Folded Leaf* I sensed an animus against the father of a greater maturity than the adolescent of the novel could express, and received it as unresolved anger at his father for remarrying when his "real" wife was dead, helpless against it.

Maxwell's father did remarry when Maxwell was young, mine not until I was twenty, and even at that age I sensed the Grimm pall of a stepmother intruding on our family life, which was barely beginning to resettle.

My father said he appreciated the poems and stories I wrote in high school and at the university, but once when I was home

over a break, after his new marriage, he said my stepmother
wondered whether it wouldn't be wise, if I wanted to write, to
first find a job to support myself, and then write in my spare
time. I wanted to say, "What do you think?" but was so clotted
with anger I couldn't speak. He did say, later, that he could see
why she thought that but wouldn't stand in the way of what I
wanted to do, and I began to see how carefully he had to weigh
her side against ours, as he weighed the aspirations and the ability of students who came to talk to him against their potential
to make a mark of any kind.

Maxwell's father, an insurance executive, could not make
sense of Maxwell's wish to write (so Maxwell said), and wondered whether writing was a respectable profession for an adult,
a *man*. Maxwell was wounded by this and only after decades
at the *New Yorker* could his father accept the career he chose,
somewhat reassured. Mine exulted in every publication.

Every son senses he is less than his father, less monumental,
less capable or patient or wise, even less profane, if his father
was. Maxwell became reconciled to his father a while before I
met him, and when he mentioned him tears ran. The first story
of his I read in the *New Yorker*, after I moved to the city, was
about a father and son; the son Edward, home on a visit, sits on
a couch as his father talks:

> Edward, floating, suspended, not quite anywhere, felt the
> safety in his father's voice, and a freedom in talking to him
> that he had never had before, not merely with his father
> but perhaps not even with anybody.

When I told Maxwell how much I liked the story, he said,
"I laid my father to rest in his grave with it." He wore a sign of

that, as in Gogol, in the form of an overcoat once his father's. His stepmother gave it to him after his father died, and for as long as I knew Maxwell he wore it from the first fall chill into the spring, although it was too big by two sizes and he was a natty dresser, circumspect and neat, without the antique mismatches or disarrangement young people note with such disdain in men they categorize as old.

Maxwell felt an early story of mine needed more detail about a character at its center, a grandfather similar to mine, and asked me up to his office and had me sit on a couch he used for naps (from 1:00 to 2:00 he was unavailable), upholstered in a silver-white fabric, had me take off my suit jacket, take off my shoes, and lie down and draw on his night-black eye mask, and said, "Relax. Drift back." He asked questions about my grandfather, then asked about my mother, who didn't appear in the story, and her face stormed down over me from the dark and I heard him saying, "Are you all right? Are you with me?" I was sitting in the brilliance of upper-level sunlight, twenty stories above Manhattan.

"Goodness, you frightened me," he said. "I had the feeling you weren't coming back."

I could remember his early questions, then her, and no more after that until I was blinking back the bright sun.

"I'll never presume to do that again," he said, and a year later, after I spent a week in the hospital when a dissociative episode ended in a minor breakdown and went to see him, my head shaved as if to blazon its vulnerability, he wiped at a tear with his index finger and said, with a grieved glance at the couch, "I'm so sorry. Remind me as often as necessary never to do that again. Say, 'Don't imagine you can do that. Ever.'"

· · ·

I was angry about my mother's absence until I realized (the second I started setting this sentence down) that she is so integrated into my personality I might as well be she. Does that mean I objectify my father, or view him through her? I'm not burrowing farther away, I hope, but further in, and when I think of you, Joseph, and our relationship, it's the winter of 1997 and we're staggering in our struggling mode of locomotion through the snow. I was so fixed on what we had to do to keep the place and the family intact I barely acknowledged you and never thought of how we handled complex work with hardly a word between us, since we knew each other's moves and natures so well. All it took was a glance or a nod.

Have I swung this way because I imagine I'll find a greater unity, a better route, in our relationship than in the ones with Maxwell and my father?

It began in Forest Park, a blue-collar suburb of Chicago, in July 1977. You were born in the master bedroom of the house we were renting. I was present, trying to aid the obstetrician, Dr. White, whose father wrote the manual on emergency childbirth that Cook County police carry in their patrol cars. I boiled water and did whatever he asked as your arrival grew difficult, your mother on her side, on her hands and knees, and at last on her back as you appeared.

Dr. White looked as soaked with sweat as I felt, as she and the sheets were, and then he handed me a pair of scissors and nodded. I cut your umbilical cord. From the start I separated you from her and, as sons feel, have ever since. It's a father's duty and prerogative and fate and true, too, for all sons. You will be cut off from her.

You were packed with muscular fat in such overlapping layers Newlyn named you "Michelin Boy." She was nine, meant to be our only child, in 1960s fashion, and after you were born a friend called and said, "Now we can't have a child. Every couple is allotted one and two-thirds and you already have that, plus our one-third. We aren't having a two-thirds kid." He was being only partly facetious; he and his wife never had a child.

You would not crawl, as if the act were beneath you. You sat on your diapered rump and pulled yourself ahead with your legs, heels digging in, elbows busy as a ballroom strutter. Then one day you stood and took off in a walk as if wisdom told you it was the only proper way to negotiate. Just before that we moved to the farm, where I sit at my usual work at the desk we built, as today you celebrate your thirtieth birthday in Iraq.

You barely spoke until you were three, and by then we learned that a necessary activity for the development of the area of the brain related to speech is crawling—that muscular derivation of language advocated by Pinsky. Science now understands it as the reason infants must crawl. So I would get down on the floor and tempt you to join my crawling game. Otherwise you wouldn't. Your speech arrived with vague impediments— R for L; a comic cast to my name—and you seemed to withhold your talk, as if you knew you didn't have it quite right and weren't about to bother till you did.

You got names reversed, as with "hopper grasser," a word I use to call you up at that age, and I remember the first word you read. Your mother wrote it on a blackboard and turned to you, one arm above it like a ballet master's, the other below, framing it, a finger pointing to the *guh* sound she wanted you to reproduce but you, like a sober judge, as your Grandpa Peterson described you, spoke instead the whole word, "God."

You weren't quite four.

From the age of three you tagged along to keep an eye on my repairs and chores. It doesn't seem possible, but when you were five you helped me uproot a huge boulder from the acre feedlot I broke up, as it does not seem possible I could budge it when I study its mass between tree rows. The tractor chain I tried to hook to it kept popping loose, no matter how I dug around the boulder, so I dug deep enough to get a shoulder under it, envisioning the mad farmer in Knut Hamsun's *Growth of the Soil* dislodging and heaving loose a stone of similar improbable girth—and natives aren't the only ancient culture to revere rock as sentient; in the Book of Joshua you'll find, "And Joshua said to all the people, 'Behold, this stone shall be a witness to us, for it has heard all the words of the Lord which He spoke to us.'"

"Pull!" I shouted, as I shoved from beneath, seeing your hands grip and go white, and in a moist outpouring of the scent of soil it broke loose and slid ahead enough to hold fast. I wrapped a chain around it in a manacle grip, and the gouge it left as I dragged it behind the tractor to its resting place between trees remained for years—still there if you know where to feel in the grass with your boot.

You observed the turn of every bolt and screw I used and once when I was on my back and said, "Can you hand me that crescent wrench," you knew what I meant and set it in my hand.

You seemed divided between work outside with me and in the house, where you grew up, and at some point you would walk off as if disenchanted and I would watch you with an intimation of the depression that would consume me when you drove down the road toward a new existence in your own house, gone not for good but gone from us.

Your mother wept in her worst way, covering her eyes, tears running over her fingers.

Up to the age of four, the loveliest age in children, when they're still wholly themselves, before the world of learning and its version of what is "real" has had a chance to impinge—to that age you were mostly mine. You knew the names of my tools and equipment, and the day you decided to use them yourself, rather than merely handing them on, I was amazed at your precision and dexterity. You had taken apart and reassembled enough of your toys and a clock and kitchen machines to know the process of mechanical complexity.

You liked to shove your fists into bread dough and squeeze and knead, folding and refolding its bubbly mass with the knuckle pressure and perseverance it takes to achieve a consistent texture—ours always whole wheat freshly ground from our organic grain—and you were often in the house a half day each week to help your mother bake bread. I disliked those days and would wonder in a wild way whether too much pleasure in baking was healthy for a boy—you know, a *male*.

Ruth and Laurel arrived and when they were old enough to help in the house, you were running the riding mower and planning to pilot a rig of your own in the field. I now know that domestic chores are a necessity to anybody who hopes for a sane disposition, the only way to keep in touch with the essentials—nutrition and cleanliness and the stabilizing influence they have at the heart of life, and your mother was always grateful for your help. She baked eight loaves of bread every Saturday, besides pastries and delicacies in between, including madeleines and croissants and lefse.

A moment that might seem inevitable arrived, since my driven hurry causes carelessness, but it seemed the natural outworking of a situation one day. You were riding on the tractor in the fields with me by the time you were four, a demand you made for the help you were the rest of the time. You probably didn't put it that way, but why shouldn't you share in the motorized activity that seemed such fun?

I strapped you to the tractor seat, in the piloting position you preferred, where you could have your hands on the wheel. There was room on the tractor platform for me to stand and negotiate the actual turns. The strap I used went across your hips and around the back of the seat, a cowboy belt with a buckle that hooked into punched holes, so I could secure you well. No falls could come when we were pulling a disk with slanted gangs of eighteen-inch circular blades polished to a knife's edge, tearing into the soil behind, or a plow with its heavy packer and drill, or a cultivator.

It was a cultivator that day, and it kept plugging with weeds and stubble, just as one did our first year on the place—the trash farmers hate. A method Sunny's father used, besides lighting piles on fire, was a fire drag, as he called it—a harrow with tires laid across it he set ablaze with gasoline and then drove off, leaving a burning trail of melted rubber dribbling down. You

don't fire-drag on a windy day, and I've noticed since the long
lengths of hookup chains neighbors use.

It wasn't windy that day, so I dropped a match into the weeds
jamming the cultivator, hopped up on the tractor beside you,
and took off. Just as the flames started to climb with an ignition
like gasoline, as weeds will, a gust of wind hit from behind and
the heat was like a hammer blow. I bent forward but couldn't
escape its scorch. I swung the tractor wide, cutting the throttle,
and the wind shifted just right to hit us with heat again from
behind. The tractor killed.

"Dad," you started crying, "*Dad!*" The seat sat farther back
from where I stood and the cultivator hung in such a close
hookup the flames were leaping at your hair. I pulled you forward,
getting my body between, and reached for the buckle, unable
to open my eyes from the heat, unable to take much more,
about to jump free. But couldn't, with you tied down. The belt
buckle was silver, with an oval of turquoise at its center that
cracked so badly I removed it, and the hook so long it seemed
impossible to free you as I strained forward and pressed against
you to shield you from the heat, my fingernails about to melt, it
seemed, while I kept forcing myself not to jump, and then I had
it loose and leaped off the front of the tractor and got far down
the field in case the gas tank blew up, hair singed, legs quaking,
holding you so close I had to let up so you could breathe.

The fire burned out, sparing the tractor, with only bubbly
scorches over its rear tires. I carried you across the fields, the
back of my hands scarlet and stinging, and we arrived at the
same place in the yard where I once believed I had a glimpse of
Eden. I was spared the sight of a serpent but knew now I was
on different ground. I was in my late thirties, a father, which

meant not only that you and your sisters were my children but that I inhabited a state you took as eternal, since you arrived with it in place—a state or role or office I could not define or fill and had to prod myself to realize was always present before you every day: *Dad*.

When you became a necessary help, completing repairs that allowed me to remain in the field or going a round or two while I watched and rested, a prescient moment arrived. You were eight or nine, getting a piece of machinery ready to hook up, and when I drove over and got off the tractor, I saw a lump on your forehead. Besides that, your lower lip was cut and bleeding.

"What happened?" I asked, distressed by the way you tried to hide the cut.

"I was lowering the jack and its handle started jumping and hit me here."

It was an equipment jack and if you lowered it while it supported a machine, it ratcheted down rapidly under the weight, flinging its pipe handle up and down, unless you hung on. Had I warned you? I wondered. Did I want any more of this? Could I handle seeing you injured? Was this the place for us? Was it mere selfishness that settled me here?

By then I had a job in the East, at a university where I taught over the academic year. We could give up the farm and move East. I was tenured. Your mother and I talked about the possibility, and when you and your sisters got wind of it you rose in protest. You didn't want to go back East one more time and submitted a drawing of cars and trucks with blaring horns balanced against the quiet of the farm. But we went back. We returned to the farm only over the summer.

. . .

One Sunday afternoon as the slant of light affirmed to the listening landscape the onset of fall, you and the girls and your mother and I lay down for a nap. We had spent the weekend packing a U-Haul trailer for our trip East, already speeding up our pace after a summer at a slowed and agreeable rate, when I woke to a blundering commotion at the door and heard cries and whimpering from Ruth.

"*What?*" I called from our bed.

"Help! *Dad!* Our barn's on fire!"

In a clatter of clothes your mother and I were dressed and out the door and I saw gray-black clouds billowing from the sliding door on the side of the barn near the house. A neighbor had rolled up a dozen round bales for us and we had stored them and a stack of square bales on the concrete floor of the drive-through. I ran to the door to slide it shut and saw a half-dozen fire extinguishers scattered across the floor, close to the round bales that were burning with such heat I had to back away. The door was hot.

"Get the garden hose!" I cried. "What *happened?*"

"We were trying out your lighter."

"My lighter?"

"Up on top of the refrigerator. It was Joseph's idea!"

I probably used the worst constructions a father can, as in "What's *wrong* with you?" or "How could you *do* this?" or "How could you be so stupid!" while trying to figure how to put the fire out. The asphalt shingles on this side of the barn were smoking and a gush of such heat came from the open door I had to turn and run. My hands were shaking so badly I couldn't get the hose on a spigot and had you run around to try to find enough lengths of hose to reach the barn.

By now the roof was on fire, shingles and rafters giving off such heat I could feel it at the house a hundred yards away, and we gathered under a tree and watched. A section of the roof above the bales collapsed and your sisters screamed.

"Just thank God you're all right," I said, and realized my shaking was fear at the harm that could have come when I saw the fire extinguishers you tried to use, carried to the barn from the basement of the house and the garage-granary.

Your mother was on the phone to the volunteer fire department a dozen miles off when the right side of the barn erupted, flames climbing through a gaping hole in the roof, and I remembered I decided to park my tractor on the far side of the bales, for safekeeping over the winter. I listened for its gas tank to blow. But the roar of burning and a wind raised by its heat reverberated like a hurricane.

A white fence attached to this side of the barn, part of a pen for loading cattle, started to burn. It was eight feet tall, built of two-by-tens nailed in solid vertical abutment, and its other end was attached to a garage-granary. If the fence kept burning at the speed it was gaining from the wind, the garage-granary would go, and two other buildings were close enough to catch. The entire center of the barn, with its thirty-foot roof, was ablaze with such consuming heat I couldn't get near enough with a hose to wet the fence.

Our closest neighbor, from the top of the hill a mile off, came tearing into the yard in his pickup and must have taken in the situation at a glance. He laid on his horn, tearing across the lawn, over the center of our circular drive, and hit the fence head on, blasting it apart, pieces flying from both sides of his pickup. He got stuck on a section of it when he tried to back up to escape the heat, revved the engine and lunged forward, and then came roaring back in a swerving action, leaping the fallen section, and braked to a stop in the middle of the yard. When he got out he had to hold up an arm to ward off the heat, so he got in his pickup and backed farther off.

The nearest neighbor to the south, Kenny Kibbel, came sliding into the yard in his pickup, jumped out, and ran over just as I was about to lay into you again for the foolish act of fiddling with my lighter, ruining our best building, my favorite, and said, "Larry, I don't think you should punish them, or say anything more. They feel bad enough. Look."

Streaks of tears stained your soot-darkened face, and when the central roof collapsed you wailed with the girls. After all I said in anger, I saw the loss was as great to you as me and maybe worse, since it was the only barn on the only place you knew from the day you could walk, as much a place of retreat for you as me, your place to play and hide. In twenty minutes the collapse was complete, with only flattened timbers ablaze, and when the firemen arrived all they could do was douse the smoking embers. The tractor was black, its tires wiry smoking shreds.

Ivan and Enid drove in behind the fire truck and didn't get out of their car. They parked a ways back and wept so hard they had to pull out handkerchiefs. They never commented on you or the cause or condemned your behavior—however they might classify the curiosity in your susceptible nature that led to acts of bravado and daring. You were lighting the wispy outer layers of round bales and one got away from you, as you explained, years later.

I said more than once in the midst of a meal, "You children have one duty, and only one. What is it?"

"To obey—*Obey!*" you all chimed in.

"The three," your mother often called you, a force gathered against her, as when, Joseph, you went around on all fours for months, perhaps due to my crawling training, barking and snapping at her and eating from the dog dish in a metamorphosis she hated, while Ruth and Laurel went galloping around the house on hands and toes, butts in the air, neighing and rising on hind legs to paw at her.

You were our "second family" to outsiders, because of the gap in age between Newlyn and you, with your arrivals at two-year intervals, and the ones who suffered most were at either end—Newlyn, forlorn in the distance between the three of you and us, not yet an adult and often left in charge of you, our "live-in babysitter," as she put it; and Laurel, led to our creepy Poe basement where you and Ruth shut off the lights and yelled, "There's a monster!" and ran upstairs, leaving her in the dark. I said the sufferers were at either end, but over the years the weight seemed to fall most in the middle, where Ruth sensed she resided, neither here nor there, yet the most ambitious, left at the loose ends of fleeting identity.

Behind your tears was the look of terror that comes with fear of oneself, and a tangent fear and remorse for Ruth, your accomplice. I took it as fear of me as much as anything and went into the bedroom and buried my face in a pillow and, in the manner of the Berns, in Dakota lingo, bawled my eyes out.

Fire for fire, I thought, and who or what was damaged most? I had endangered you by all I'd let slip or hadn't sought for you, a son without a father to steer by.

Here at the desk you and I built I sit up as if from that bed, myself at last, with the startling thought that you're in Iraq, and then: Joseph, *you're* a father now.

7

Child as Father

The Wordsworth poem that begins "My heart leaps up when I behold/A rainbow in the sky" contains a line people often quote, "The Child is father of the Man," meaning you are my father, Joseph. In the concluding couplet Wordsworth adds, "And I could wish my days to be/Bound each to each by natural piety." William Blake, the visionary poet who also etched dreamlike engravings during Wordsworth's era, wrote in the margin of his copy of the Wordsworth poem, next to that couplet, "There is no such Thing as Natural Piety Because The Natural Man is at Enmity with God."

Blake was at enmity with Wordsworth, as further marginal notes reveal, and Wordsworth, who seemed unable to decide whether he was a philosopher of nature, a natural theologian, or a poet, was, according to contemporary accounts other than his sister's, stiff and distant and more enamored of himself the more he wrote, rather than the reverse, as you will discover in Blake and Donne and Herbert and many poets who are near or present contemporaries, such as John Crowe Ransom and Theodore Roethke and Joseph Brodsky and Anne Sexton and Marilyn Nelson and Carolyn Forché. Each has a singular way of setting the sum of the meaning of a poem outside the confines of self, some in a manner of self-immolation.

They are writers of a higher order.

If Wordsworth hadn't felt the need to add the concluding couplet, his poem's suggestive truth might carry into our age with persevering clarity: *The child is father of the man.* Think of that. The point of application is bound to seem diminishing, even demeaning, to parents.

One summer your mother and I were in Canada with New-lyn, our only child then, for relief from a book I became obsessed with, *Beyond the Bedroom Wall,* and were lying on the bank of a secluded lake, listening to waves raised by a wind spatter stones a canoe-length from our feet. The measure was our beached canoe. We needed the refreshment of a retreat but hadn't given up the pressures and conflicts that caused the need, and suddenly we were caught up in an argument of such heat we had to sit up—so mundane I can't remember the content—another of the arguments that afflicted our marriage, especially its first years, until one or the other realized it was possible to make room for the other without a sovereign self being undermined, allowing reconsideration, rearrangement, even compromise, if not growth and reconciliation, to take place.

Not on this day. We were holding out with the hammer-and-tongs bravado of non-Socratic wrangling. Newlyn sat off

at a distance, tearing up grass in her frustration, and then in the
swift sleight of a child she was in front of us, red-faced, her arms
at her sides, fists clenched, and in a voice like ours she cried,
"Would you two stop *arguing?*"

She was four, the two of us thirty, and we looked up like
children chastened, trying to formulate the excuse that goes,
It wasn't me . . .

About this time your mother and I read *I'm OK, You're OK,*
during a stretch of such suggestibility it seemed we couldn't ask
each other or Newlyn (or any of the rest of you, as you came along)
anything, or even offer a suggestion, without adding, "OK?"

I met your mother on the Urbana campus of the University
of Illinois, in a crowd of 38,000, counting grad students and
faculty, and not the crew necessary to keep it running. She was
studying foreign languages and political science with a goal of
entering diplomatic service. She wanted to know several languages so she could serve in an embassy overseas, perhaps as aide
to a diplomat. She also imagined the fascination of acting as a
tutor to the children of an ambassador and becoming a member
of a high-ranking household in the Russian tradition—the sort
of person invited to social gatherings hosted by international
diplomats, even royalty, as in Norway or Denmark, Britain or
the Netherlands.

Then she met me. That's how her parents saw it. She met
me and an earlier interest in writing and painting resurfaced—
creative abilities that apparently satisfied her more than societal
interconnections and travel—although it took years for her to
forgive me, as I recall it, for thwarting her potential. We were
ambitious in the manner of the 1960s, which meant money
didn't matter, or anyway we would never "sell out," as it was

said then. She continued writing and drawing and found she
had a gift for photography. She tutored Newlyn so well she was
reading at the age of four.

How can I say the next, except as it was? We separated and
lived apart, for reasons I'll explain, and she enrolled Newlyn in
a private Christian school in Chicago. We were reunited a year
and a half later, and Newlyn was so altered I felt I was the child
to her parent. Before, she was withdrawn in a meditative way,
which may have registered her mistrust in me as a father, and
I wanted to know what had happened or what she was learning that had changed her. She was a seven-year-old with the
joyful composure and confidence of a successful adult. I don't
think I asked her the question directly, but the change was so
remarkable I knew it arrived from another realm, a spiritual
transformation.

The school offered courses by correspondence, so when we
moved to North Dakota, a dozen miles from any town, Newlyn
continued her schooling by correspondence in our farmhouse.
The first two weeks Enid, retired teacher and administrator,
came out to advise us and taught a lesson or two from the couch,
where she sat with such poise, spine upright, she seemed hardly
to adhere to the edge of its cushions.

In less than a month we learned that our teaching, even with
Enid present, was illegal. That's right. North Dakota was one
of the last states to keep on its books what was in effect a child-
labor law, or a surer way than my father's for getting immigrant
children to school, that is, from the age of seven to sixteen every
child in the state had to attend public school, no exceptions.
The parochial schools were grandfathered in when the law was

passed, but were required to hire state-certified teachers, teach the state-approved curricula, and meet state-mandated hours every day, besides other state demands.

I went to the local superintendent, who had sent out the sheriff, whose wife was on the school board, to find out why Newlyn wasn't in school. Public school employees and board members were commissioned as truant officers by the same law. I looked it up in the Century Code, a compilation of state laws, before I could believe it was true. I was testy and resistant and the superintendent said I better go see the local state's attorney.

I said to the attorney, "I don't feel we're beyond the pale of the law," intending to mention the U.S. Constitution, and he said, "You're way beyond the pale! She's been out of school for three weeks and if she's not there on Monday I'm going to throw you in jail for thirty days and fine you two-hundred-and-fifty dollars a day for every day she's not there!" This, too, was the law. I was on medication after a bout of confused distress from low blood sugar, and not well. I called the headmaster of the school in Chicago, the largest correspondence school of its kind at the time, and he said this happened so seldom, and never with such force, he would give me the names of two constitutional lawyers. I called my editor Michael at Farrar, Straus, where my next book was contracted, because of the upset this was causing to my schedule, already slowed by illness, and he said, "It sounds like Siberia! Do you want me to get in touch with *Time* or *Newsweek* or the *Times* and see if they'll send out a stringer to cover this? It's a human rights issue!"

What we needed was Nat Hentoff, savvy enough to intuit

the effect of Bob Dylan in the first piece written on him, which appeared in the *New Yorker*.

I decided no. I was ill and didn't want to brand myself as a troublemaker in a community we were only beginning to get acquainted with, mostly through teaching at home. And people were only doing their duty according to the law. "Get the legislature to change the law if you don't like it!" the state's attorney said. "That's the process." It was.

I tried to envision how my father would react. He had decided, with no preface or warning, to retire early, two years before he died, and when I asked why, he said, "The unions seem to me about to ruin teaching. It's becoming too much what you make rather than what the students learn."

On the night before the day Newlyn was supposed to be in school, your mother and I sat at the round table we discovered in an antique shop in Brooklyn Heights and now had here, with an inlay of bird's-eye maple encircling it, and went over the routes we might take, including the possibility of my spending time in jail, since I was the responsible parent, as the state's attorney informed me. Our further concern was how the law would affect you, Joseph, at the age of seven.

I felt as vulnerable and divided as the day we decided to move from New York, a difficult decision, considering my relationship with Maxwell and Bob De Niro and others, besides business associations, access to editors and my agent and my publisher, and a tax accountant who kept us true. Then one morning I woke and looked down at Newlyn, who was born a month early, before we had a room ready, asleep in a dresser drawer, an improvised cradle, beside our bed, and realized we couldn't remain in the city, for her sake.

After the *Times* report on breathing city air, I was aware of how, when I returned from Manhattan, I coughed up black crud or, if I blew my nose, left black streaks, and I couldn't submit her to that, so the question was where we would move, among the variations we considered—no plan except perhaps to buy a house up the coast, in Maine, if my first novel sold as we hoped—and then my father called to offer a suggestion: Why didn't we store our belongings at his place until we found a house of our own? Mary and Marce, my younger sisters, were in college.

"Why not live here? This house is so big—the one we always should have had. I come home from school and rattle around in it expecting to see one of you kids. You and Carole and Newlyn are welcome to stay as long as you want."

As you know, I go backward to move ahead, and a cross-weave of the past threading through the present to affect the future was on the go again, back and forth, over and under the contradictory routes we might choose to educate you (you grew up that quick, as you know, already gone), unable to settle on any in unanimity of satisfaction. I trust Care's instincts, I thought. What is best for her? If she could tutor diplomats' children, why not ours? Sparks of argument probably flared. Language here leaves me.

Because at about that moment Newlyn came stepping down the stairs from her second-story bedroom and walked over to the table, looking abashed. "Why don't you take me in to the school in town tomorrow," she said. "It's all right. I'll be OK."

"The Child is father of the Man" is not sexist. It suggests that the person responsible for a decision isn't necessarily the adult who may not endure beyond its effects. The ability to rise to a situation and, even better, resolve it to entire satisfaction, is creative, which was Wordsworth's clue.

The basic impulse in children is creative. Watch one at play. He lays out roads for his trucks. She builds barns or castles for her horses and cattle. And as with any inborn instinct, a contrasting opposite rises—the tower of blocks knocked over with a shout of glee, in a hint of the terrified fascination for fires and accidents and the gnawing excess of the perverse. In order for the tower of blocks to fall, the body to be broken, the building to go up in flames, the drunk to drool in the backseat, however, there must be a created form that is being broken or taken down.

That original form supersedes any destruction or erosion or attacks or assaults on it, and when adults act like children, children act exactly like those adults.

I tried to be a father to you through your youth and hoped to carry on the type of teaching prescribed to Israel in the book of Deuteronomy—how they were to love the One-You-Can't-Name with all their heart and soul and might and speak of Him as they worked in the house or walked beyond it, from the time they got up in the morning until they went to bed at night. This is creative work, with the implication that children watch what you do and learn from it as well as they hear what you say, and more often do as you do rather than practice what you preach.

So how did this relate to digging through frozen manure in a barn pen, I thought, one bitter morning when I was doing that, trying to locate a pipe that had burst underground and added to the sloppy freeze before I shut it off. You were at my side as usual, at the wiggly age of three, trying not to get in my way as I wondered how I could speak about the situation in terms of a

Holy One when you grabbed my pant leg and yelled, "For his own glory in his ear!"

"What?" I straightened up and looked around.

You pointed your mitten with such intensity I could see your finger through the weave of its knitting and looked and saw a fence-crawling heifer in a corner of the barn. "For his own glory in his ear, Dad!" you cried again, insistent. "For his own glory in his ear!"

I saw the yellow ID tag hanging from the heifer's ear, the "humane" way to brand, though you punch a hole in an ear to do it, and realized it was the same size and color as the children's catechism your mother was helping you memorize as you sat in her lap, and you were up to the second question, *Why did God make all things?* "For His own glory" was the answer, the text from a yellow book the size of the yellow tag attached to the God-made thing's ear. I sighed and leaned on my shovel, heir to another lesson from a child.

The Chiclets of the keyboard chatter like my teeth in a freeze of forty-below as I think of the times when we were on a transcontinental trip of the sort we took every fall and spring, to the East and back, the three of you accelerating into boisterous upheaval in the rear of the station wagon, and if I yelled at you to quiet down, Laurel would drop asleep. It was on those trips I noticed this, probably because she was only an arm's length away. The next time I raised my voice she went down as if dealt a knockout blow. And I understood that the tongue, with its creative ability, its power to heal, is also a razor able to slice others to ribbons of living death.

It may be best to leave in silence the unspoken warnings children give parents about their harmful behavior: a sideways look of shame. Everybody is either a child or an adult, and some are both, as I am, I admit, Joseph, pursued by a dead mother and overseen by a dead father. My existence is an extended excursion to discover how deep in my past their deaths are fixed, or if I'm finally free enough of them in the present to fall into the future where, suspended, I'm bathed in the endlessness existence actually is.

Parents are on the receiving end, too, and the worst news, in my view, arrives by telephone. The call came from your mother, out of breath, who said, "It's Joseph. He's terribly hurt. It's bad."

"What do you mean?"

"The horse he was riding went wild when we had the saddle half off. He spun and the saddle hit Joseph and knocked him down and the horse went over the top of him."

"How bad?" My words barely emerge.

"He's breathing now. But he isn't conscious. I have to go. The ambulance is here. Get to the hospital to meet us!"

I had a sense of how my father felt when he got a call from my Grandma Johnston telling him to hurry to the hospital because my mother's life was ebbing—a cellular rush toward every extremity that caused me to feel I was giving way at the edges. You and your mother and Ruth and Laurel were riding at a friend's ranch, I knew that, and only that, and went on a run to the oldest of our station wagons, with a 400-hp engine, and made the twenty miles in fifteen minutes.

The ambulance was backing up to the emergency entrance. I ran over and your mother and I connected in an embrace of such solid contact we seemed to fly through each other. The ambulance doors opened. You were on a stretcher, in a neck brace, your face ivory, eyes closed, an oxygen mask covering your mouth. Why is it injured children look entirely undone, frail shadows of a former being? We took hold of you on both sides as they wheeled you in and had to wait. You were breathing with a gasp to each breath, as if every breath barely came, but your eyelids never squeezed tight or wavered. You were so deep inside yourself, in another existence, our voices didn't reach you.

I touched a swelling, the skin torn away, near your temple, and your mother said it was where the saddle hit. "I think. I ran to him and said, 'Breathe, Joseph, *breathe!*' over and over. It seemed he never would so I took him in my arms, which maybe I shouldn't have done, should I, and kept telling him to breathe and finally he did, with a gasp I felt all the way through me."

She was wiping at tears with the back of her hand as she spoke, and it wasn't until this fall, 2005, two decades down the line, that she was able to tell me that during those critical seconds she sensed a presence and glanced up and saw a malign face leering at her from between the bars of the corral. Then it was gone.

The emergency room nurse, our friend Phyllis, put her hand over your forehead where the hairline was skinned back, perhaps from a hoof, and whispered, "Oh, Joseph, I'll be praying for you." Dr. Hsu arrived in a rush and checked your eyes and said he couldn't see hemorrhaging and inserted an IV and a breathing tube, and from a quick X-ray saw three broken ribs—those groans with each breath, pain I now know.

But Dr. Hsu couldn't do any more, as if baffled by your state, although he saw your turning to throw up as positive—"A great sign!" He told the ambulance crew to take you to Bismarck.

The law didn't allow us to ride with you, so we followed in the station wagon your mother drove off in to take you riding, the girls settled with friends, Newlyn at a job in the East to help fund her schooling in Massachusetts.

So we drove with you hidden from us, the swirls of upset in me feeling as weighty as nickels and quarters. Your mother and I were reciting the Lord's Prayer, over and over, for the eighty-mile drive.

They took more X-rays and a CAT scan and decided against a tracheotomy, because you seemed to be breathing well enough now, and we followed your stretcher to a room in the ICU, with a single bed at its center and enough space for a crowd of twenty, besides a bank of monitoring equipment. A doctor and nurse attached electrodes and pressure cuffs to every area of your body. The nurse inserted a catheter, writhing at the task in one so young. You didn't register a response.

The wait began. X-rays and CAT scans didn't reveal any abnormality other than the fluid that collects after a heavy blow, so they inserted a new IV into your other arm to counteract that. We were allowed to stay in the room and we held your hands, one on each side. The space in the room allowed for the passage of specialists and interns, sometimes four or five, and we had to step back as one more stethoscope was set down on you, your eyes pried open and examined once again, your mouth pulled open and peered into, all this performed on your inert body.

"Does everybody here have to do this?" your mother asked of a group going through the same process once again. When they left, we each took a hand of yours and talked to you and prayed.

I said, "I know you're there. If you can hear me, give my hand a squeeze!" Nothing. "We're here. We're staying with you. We're right here. We won't leave."

Your mother kissed your hand, leaned in and kissed your face laden with attachments, including now a feeding tube.

One pediatrician suspected brainstem damage, or some involvement with the brainstem, due to the doctors' inability to raise certain reflexes when they tapped or scraped at you. But he and a neurologist who examined you thought that was contradicted by the way your autonomic nervous system kept up—though your breathing was shallow, slow, your heartbeat slowed, your blood pressure low, all the signs of a person *in a coma*. Your state now had a name. We would see what tomorrow brought, they said. This continued for three days, the point at which you should have awakened, they said.

My thoughts were swirling in the wobbly orbit of moths circling lamplight, some sailing off in the dark and swinging back with a tinge of the alien, seeking a place to rest. Every act in my life that might have caused your accident replayed with a glow of accusation, at the center of it all my drinking, now mostly in the past but reappearing enough to mar moments or cause you to question my stability (my *worth*, I thought), so I would forswear alcohol, I said inside. And beneath this my backstory, internal when it wasn't spoken, kept up: *I know you're there. I'm with you. We'll do all we can to help. I will not leave you. I won't let you go. I know the good work God started in you will be brought to completion. He won't abandon you. I won't. People all over are praying for you.*

We heard from so many, from the East where I taught and states along the way and states far west that I was surprised to learn how many people prayed, or said they did. Pastors visited and prayed. Day four came, with growing pessimism in the assembly of doctors about your emerging intact, if you emerged. *I know you're there. I know you. I know the good work . . .* Your blood pressure dipped below reason and finally I had to summon the courage to say to myself, If this is the way it will be, it will be. But I won't give up. I won't let you go. I'll never leave you.

Day five, and your mother is sure she senses a response in you, in your hand and your expression, and the doctor who attends you most of the day stares at her with the distance of a professional Skeptic. A group of young people gather in the hall, friends of yours from church, and we give them permission, as we're required, to visit you. They gather at the bed and give greetings that sound boisterous after so many days of silence, and one of them says, "Should we sing?" They decide on a psalm they know and sing it together, their high voices in unison, a few taking harmony, and in my state the sound is so angelic I'm overcome, as if this is your end.

Your eyelids flutter. They open, your eyes vague and dim in a search for the source of the sound.

"Hey, Joseph," one of the boys says, and your eyes swing in his direction, in recognition. You attempt to smile.

You wet the corners of your mouth with your tongue. Your mouth moves and I see a compression of your throat to speak.

No words come. The feeding tube.

I ask the doctor to remove the tubes and when he sees you're awake and does his tests to make sure you are, he agrees, since the feeding tube, he says, is causing your stomach to bleed. Still you can't speak. We watch you try, but no words arrive.

"Don't worry," I say, "that will come too," and you sink back to sleep from the effort you've made.

· · ·

The next day they move you to a regular room and when we sleep, we sleep sitting up or lying beside you. Your body is as creaky as an old man's, not counting the broken ribs, and you can't sit. Physical therapists work on you every few hours, and after two days of this your mother asks if we can't do the exercises at home; she has a sense that the farm, your love, will heal you. You can sit and you attempt to walk with us on each side, but your legs are stiff and flail in odd ways. If we promise to continue the exercises at home, the doctor says, yes, he will release you. So we take you home.

You still haven't spoken, although faint sounds rise from you. We grip the back of your belt to help you walk. The family is in mourning—Ruth and Laurel especially, with the planner and encourager of their escapades absent—as if at a wake. I try to pray at meals, but such bitter anger clots my throat I want to hack it up. Instead we say in unison the Lutheran grace a relative taught Newlyn, and at one of the meals an odd sound chirps in. Your mother is out of her chair and has you in her arms. "Joseph," she says. "You're talking!"

"You prayed!" the girls cry.

Your face, blank for so many days, alters as if you want to smile, and you say, "Yes."

It's an odd voice, higher than before, scratchy and out of tune, as if the tubes cut grooves in your vocal chords. You can speak only in monosyllables. It's past the time when I should be in the East teaching, but the farm seems to exert the healing effect your mother suspected, and I'm too worn out to drive. I make an agreeable promise to be back in two weeks and hire a pair of graduate students to teach my classes.

· · ·

And since we're here, I feel there's no use being idle. I might as well fence the southwest front of our land, a job I've meant to do—wires and a section of posts torn down by the renter under the Berns, in a malign rush to get his rig in the field. I hitch up a stoneboat Newlyn and I built when we fenced the front pasture, so we could keep a horse on the place, the new fencing meant to be an addition to that, and when I start pulling out of the yard you appear from the door somehow on your own at the sound of the tractor and with your gestures let me know you want to come along.

So I set you down, so thin now, on the stoneboat among the fencing tools and rolls of barbwire and start off, taking the easy course down the road and then back into the front of the farm at a gate that still exists. You sit and watch as I work on the fence and seem content with that. Once when I look up, you're staring across the farm and I remember how you said this year you didn't want to leave, didn't want to go back, didn't want me to teach anymore, didn't think it was right, and I believe I sat you on my lap, though you were getting old for that (now I've been holding you that way again), and said, "Well, right now the teaching helps support the farm. So we have to go back."

Then I remembered the first spring we were here, when I had Newlyn help me build the stoneboat, a platform of two-by-eights on four-by-four skids, to ease my rolling of stones onto it, those I could roll, and then loaded it with fencing equipment and told Newlyn she had to help fence the front pasture, and after a week of work that must have seemed unrelenting to her, our hands and arms scabbed from barbs, we were done. On a morning in early May, her birthday, I asked her to come with me to the pasture to check on something and discovered it was white with fog. "Wait here," I said, and located

the horse I'd bought for her and realized I couldn't have staged
a better moment, seeing her expression as we appeared out of
the mist like a mirage, and said, "Here's your horse."

"Oh, Dad!" she cried. "Can we afford it?"

Now out of the mist of my grief I study you as you stare over
the farm. You revolve on the stoneboat and look at me with the
expression of the sober judge your grandfather saw in you, and
you must sense something of the state I'm in because you say
in the longest speech I've heard from you since we've returned,
"It's OK, Dad. I'm OK. See?"

INTERIM

One,
THE SKINNY,
a backstory,

Opens on the February morning of 2000 after the fluttery film of me being trundled down a line of ambulances appears and burns through, as we pack for our trip to Arizona. The snow keeps up its heavy fall and I stick out my tongue and catch crumpling spangles that taste of cistern water. I wanted to be on the road before noon, but the car is still in the drive at 4:00 PM. I blame it on Care, but it's me, too, working on my talk, and it's the packing, a bookish task of arrangement that reminds me of the years in New York when I read a novel a day, so enamored of writing and its practitioners I woke to the air of a Turgenev hunt, shaved with a razor like a character from Cather, brewed thick black coffee in honor of Colette, and sat at an oak table studying my mug and its reflection as if I were Tolstoy at the edge of the allure of his peasant existence, although he was a landed aristocrat, a count, of a gentrified century past—the coffee sending me into such interpolated literary loop-the-loops I felt I was about to grab Shakespeare by the hips.

I pause for these imagistic onslaughts, sifting through each, and by the time I have everything packed in the trunk, with odd pieces crammed into slots and crannies, night is descending in deepening layers of snow in an illusion of huge wings settling and shadowing the yard. The flakes take on sheen from the lit windows of the house, and my morning vision of ambulances idling along a road flickers close. *I packed too much*, I think. Nine hundred pounds, I judge, from boxes I weighed, paper the heaviest.

The lid of the trunk is taut, bowed, all spare space stuffed, the rear floor and half the backseat stacked with boxes and overnight bags, barely room for Laurel's feet, the boat-like hood of the Lincoln canting up—lots of flashing headlights, I figure, from truckers who think I have my brights on.

Wind embeds snow like mail over my coat and sets the illuminated cone below our yard light swinging into such a thick descent of flakes I can't see the building on the other side. I might make the first day of the conference still, if we leave now—*I can say no,* I think, and hear the fall of flakes grow audible over my cap.

A clump of the house door closing comes through the muffling snow, and Care, angel in the night, is in the lit front seat, Laurel the back. So I get in and hear the creaking scrawl of cold tires in frozen snow. I tell them we are *not* taking the back road, thirty miles of gravel to Kathleen Norris country, Lemmon, but our frontage road to Highway 21, then 49 south, this side of New Leipzig.

Over our four miles of gravel, though, I can barely see, partly from poor night vision this past year. Then I enter a sudden letup and swing east on 21, but within a mile, with wind rocking us, visibility goes. I'm able to guide the car by keeping its hood between the gold center stripes and neon-like shoulder line, the road beneath a snowy maze.

A semi blasts past, bronze fog lights reflecting off the swirling surface, its running lights bannering past in a digital blare, and a cloud of snow fog blinds me to both lines. I brake and ribbons of snow entering the headlights jolt to the side as I grip the wheel to keep us in line, sensing the fluttery film rise from the floor of my mind.

"We're stopping at the motel in Elgin," I say—a dozen miles off. "It's too far to go back, and if we do we'll never leave. This is a ground blizzard. I can't see."

"Just drive slow."

I hear this so often I'm ready to erupt, slogging along at thirty as I am, and from behind I feel Laurel's tension. She is the one who, when we endured the interior of a station wagon on a transcontinental trip and I gave a baleful glare at backseat behavior or, worse, raised my voice, dropped asleep, bang, as if knocked out. Now she's seventeen, a tall brunette (measured against her sisters) who plays the violin, her nerves fretted in musical fashion, and will, when parental thunderclouds gather, get groggy, grow sleepy, or cry, "Not this again!" And if our tone tends toward an argument, she starts humming in a loud voice she seems to hope will drive us off.

She also can't stand to see us smoke and can't stand smoke, so the trip will be smokeless.

.   .   .

We check in after nineteen miles, and I can't sleep, although my eyelids feel like oiled lead, nerves shot from a few miles. I'm still on the road, levitated in lines of flakes entering the lights, alert to the slightest sound, to Care's breathing, Laurel's in the bed next to us. I put a hand on Care's shoulder as if to say, *I hope to be not only on the same page but in the same sentence, in a verb*—the last months the most complicated in our thirty-some years. She goes from complimenting me in new ways to insisting, after a recent night, rare lately, of too much to drink, "You have to find help, Larry, you really do, professional or otherwise, I don't care, just do it! And not for my sake. For you!"

I empathize, I do, I say inside as if to her and then another force rolls from the moment we stood face-to-face as she said that, sailing through me like a snow-melting wind: the womanly opposite of my mother. And I sense I'm at the edge of my January abyss—*sometimes I feel like a motherless child*—whose defining feature is space so blank it could be ground zero, 9/11, leaving a gouged gap, her grave. I thought I could drag her toward light, revive her with volleys of words, pages, chapters, books, petty vain paper constructions, but she slipped back to an absence of blank blackness in blasted space. And I feel I'll follow her in womb-drawn consanguinity, unless you, Care, wholly unlike her, keep up your assured Scandinavian steadiness, your eyes on me and our children, rather than the dark-haired fiery do-it-this-second woman I carry as my mother: "It's enough to make you weep!" she would wail, and then weep, covering her face with her hands, *hoo-hooing* in a mourning dove's death throes.

Your mother, Joseph, can displace that, and if she lets up, which is the way it feels when her affection wanes (as in the country song, *Some people think I'm a loser/Because I can't get things right,/But I think I'm a winner/When you wrap me in your arms, tight)*, I'm tempted to dive in my mother's direction, a threat under all the rest in the list, as she well knows (either of the two mothers)—all this arriving in a tangled rush I can barely sort, including the country western song's classy predecessor, Yeats's lines, *When my arms wrap you round I press/upon my heart the loveliness/that has long faded from the world.*

On the internal intercom where phrases and lines for poems arrive, I hear my father declaim in the tone he uses for Shakespeare, *And all our yesterdays have lighted fools the dusty way to death!* This plays over and over, like a tape loop, until it seems I'm asleep, though not quite, since being a son, *in response to him, especially in writing,* seems insuperable, the cause of later struggles with Maxwell, which occurred mostly in silence but were braided with emotion and hard fought, or came to be, *so few examples of sonship in American writing,* rather than *the usual railing against a father,* such as mine. And in the wake of death, of *her,* wondering whether my own death would hit before I finished the book on sexual bonds beyond the confines of a bedroom wall in a family's ranks, the effrontery no one wrote about, the household sweat and pubic patches, and sensed as I worked that I was assembling the scenes I saw on a cyclorama at the back of my mind the night I sat contemplating the more than heaven or earth in *Hamlet.*

A quaking pressure came with work on the book, invading my senses with the scent of a cheap perfume Care didn't use, along with the stink of stale garage grease, as I heard on my echoing intercom voices other than the one that delivered lines of poetry, and knew I couldn't write one more word for that scene, not then, so I would set off in a new direction, barely sleeping at the onslaught, and one day saw it was the end of

January, checking the calendar like a rune, the run of the new year's colors distorted by a tightening in my mind at the thought of the date of her death, and felt she had led me to the calendar to locate the reason behind my dislocation, and realized I loved my father more than her.

For the guilt of that I couldn't find words, *what I and other sons*, too, I was sure, felt, and *father* suggested a wintry distance, as in "Our Father who art . . ." when "Dad" is what he was from the start, down the far hall at the exit door of consciousness, where words form for their tryout on my tongue—never Daddy or Pop or the euphemisms that don't address the beginning and end of who he was: *Dod.*

Which is how I hear his name arriving down the hall, over the echoing intercom, in a lineup of sounds, *Dod, Tod, Dead,* Omega to her Alpha. *Everett.* With a fondness for the actor Edward Everett Horton but no patience with the excesses of Everett Dirksen, our Illinois senator, the grossest abuser of the English language, to his mind, in public office, akin to General Douglas MacArthur, although it wasn't MacArthur's language so much (as with Dirksen, who used "fifty-cent words when a penny one would do") as his rhetorical smugness. Any tendency toward that or bombast caused him to turn aside with an "Ugh!"—his wavy hair so dark it appeared black, with the simmering look of Victor Mature and a cheerful nature women found attractive, eyebrows curved in half-round arches, so when eyeglasses with clear plastic frames were the style, worn by Groucho on *You Bet Your Life, Dod* wore a pair, too, and like that master of the comic take waggled his eyebrows to add to a punch line. It helped that he smoked cigars or a pipe, a handy prop adopted in college when he hoped to be an actor but took stock of that against providing for a family (he was about to marry *her*) and came down on teaching, first of math and history, then English and drama, exorcising his theatrical bent, besides coaching every high school sport, including women's basketball, with his athletic disposition and ability to assess an opponent. Also, perhaps not oddly—adding attributes up—he was a water witch.

He took a forked twig and at the spot on earth where it swung down or dowsed, found water, as when I watched a nine-foot sand point, a perforated cone with a pipe attached, hammered into soil at his bidding spill buckets. He located not only water, but with a length of wire in each hand, ends bent in ninety-degree grips, could walk a yard and tell you where a pipe was buried, pausing at a spot and pivoting, then stepping around until the wires in both hands swung straight out to each side: "Right here," he would say. He didn't expect pay from the people he helped, though now and then somebody handed him a dollar or two in gratitude, as it was in those days.

In the days when everybody smoked and teachers stepped out during recess for a quick one, he tended not to smoke, anyway not at school—he didn't inhale—but if he wanted a pipe he headed for the furnace room and sat with the janitor as he puffed, tapping his teeth or poking at them with the stem, not the sort to aim his pipe like a pistol to emphasize a point, and not a bearer of backstairs gossip, even after he became, as in North Dakota, principal and then superintendent and dealt with dozens of faculty and staff and hundreds of students (so we had to learn to field the gossip of others about him) but preferred the company of laborers—those who maintained the building and kept its machinery going, with an interest in the actual, not condescending theories—the employee he

most admired a carpenter and all-around repairman and custodian, though it wasn't *that*; it wasn't mirroring gender or a
male's rough skills, because women wrote to say they never
would have received an advanced degree, even finished high
school, if it weren't for him, and might well be, as one put it,
still detasseling corn—all from the several sets of society in a
small town that, to most locals, are either haves or have-nots,
although he didn't make that distinction, alert instead to individual response, her degree of attention or sudden flash in a
patch of writing, eerily intuitive about potential and adverse
effects on it, as with a couple who chauffeured their sons to
school in a Chrysler with tinted windows (you could locate two
shadows in the back craning to see out), about whom he said
once as they drove by, "They're making it all but impossible for
those boys to learn."

     His method of teaching was to lean on a rostrum and read
or recite with an actor's skill the stories and poems he liked,
avoiding lengthy discussion of symbols and theoretical intent,
which I can say because I took the only college English course in
town, his, embarrassed by the emotion he let leak into his readings, assuming it was over my mother, as I assumed when I saw
his tears after a *Masterpiece Theatre* finale or less worthy venue.
One day he read the Tennyson poem that ends, "Break, break,
break/at the foot of thy crags, O Sea!/But the tender grace of a
day that is dead/Will never return to me!" with such seething
finality the entire class sat in stunned silence.
     He carried his talent into public readings and dramatic
monologues, in vogue in the fifties, often in dialect, but not
the dialects one might imagine—an Italian accent for the guide
from *Innocents Abroad*, the correct pronunciation of French

names in an excerpt from *Les Miserables*, which he called "The Bishop's Candlesticks," but my internal intercom reproduces with greatest clarity, in a downshift to the retrograde gear of memory, the striding voice of the trooper, vowels shading toward Cockney, saying

> Oh, it's Dean, Dean, Dean,
> Where the Divel ha-yaw bean,
> Ya lash-a Rooshin leathah, Gunga Dean!

and one day he walked from the blackboard—*College English* written at its top in his Palmer-perfect penmanship—to the sunlit windows, gripping a fist behind his back and rocking in place, jabbing at the hem of his suit jacket, dreamy-eyed from a reading of Poe, "Oh, Helen, thy beauty is to me like those Nicean barks of yore!" and said from memory,

> I was a child and she was a child,
> In this kingdom by the sea,
> And we loved with a love that was more
> Than love, I and my Annabel Lee

with such subdued fervor even the dreamers sat at attention, the room charged with an atmosphere as potent as the sea, and I stared down in shame, a sting like the spray of a wave over my eyes, sure that this was how he saw himself and my mother when they were young, now that she was dead.

I flop on my back like a fish out of water, a walloped walleyed gasper, and go *One* . . .

Two,
(a reliance on numerals I resort to
when words won't work and)
THE FILM HITS,
a warning

I have to suppress from rising through the floor of my mind, sprung by death. *Three.* Dead three months from the day I turned nine and for a dozen years he didn't remarry, the only positive aspect, thank God for that and the strength that enabled him to endure, when it isn't mismanaged, because he could take you out with a swing (and once sent me skidding on my ass across the living room with a backhand to my chest like an afterthought), and his fear of his strength is the source of the tentative look he uses at home and on his students, a look that overcomes him when he does the dishes alone, and if I grab a towel to help, feeling sorry for him and angry that I do, he turns as he did at the funeral home when I found him leaning over her casket, mouth parted, eyes as liquid as in a waking dream, as if he sees her beyond the window where our reflections slide against the night and is drowning the dishes in his outpouring of grief.

An outrageous thought, as I may have thought then, but our existence in her absence is outrageous, our father our mother now, womanly, grieving, giving, clinging, pinned to his emotion like a lance his body sags from, shoulders starting to give, and once the dishes are done he goes to the side of the house that holds his bedroom, to use "the can," as he calls it, wary of our proximity to the other bathroom, and the detonations that arrive through the walls like explosives down a culvert are amusing at first, worthy of withering comment, and then attended to like utterances of his oncoming end, the five of us staring away from the television at this ultimate grief that could carry him off.

He's half absent anyhow from his focus on her, but he keeps the only order we know, cooking dinner after teaching or a day of summer labor, able to shred the morbid tableau we assume with his cry, "Here it comes! Pull my finger!" and releases a rattling flatulence over the plastic upholstery of his easy chair, willing to descend to the lowest of low comedy to revive his troupe and get their swags of belly-fat galloping in a chatter of laughter—

It's he who insists we go to catechism every Saturday and leads us in grace and reminds us to pray if he's not present, the common Catholic grace, before our dive for food, and gets us to church on time and afterward buys sweet rolls at the supermarket across the highway, so sweet they burn my teeth, the day murky and dampened by the inky Technicolor of Sunday funnies, our Sabbath solace, and through all this never loses it, as Ruth says, never kicks at things or throws them, as I have, though his anger can erupt if he catches us at mean-spirited acts, as when he sent me skidding across the living room, but subdues the anger, doesn't permit our stirring it up, seeing himself in us, perhaps (as I do in you four), rising into life faster than he does, yet of his flesh, our faults mirror images of his or, worse, the woman who bore us—breath passing away in the night—so I know the rigors and heartbreak of a single-parent family during an era when outsiders would say, "Those children have no mother!" defining our situation or, in a manner of forgiveness meant to explain another fix, "Those poor boys don't have a dad."

Ours does not drink, this alone meriting the reward of his summer trips, driving as far as New Mexico or California or New York without a stop, dazed by a force that propels him forward and, in spite of that momentum, is able to keep his habits in order and attend to us without a swig or other medication—neither as tempting as in the present, perhaps—and in all of this teaches us, along with thousands of students, how to survive.

So I can say at this juncture, older than he was when he died—

Care rolls in bed and loops an arm over me, as fast asleep as when she touched down, and gathers me close.

Now that I'm beyond the age he was when he died, I can say, If you bend to the nature of your father, whether sooner or later, you've done well, you've done *good*, you've admitted you're able to accept who you are in his eyes—the person most discerning about your weaknesses—even if some sympathetic others draw different talents from you, which you're willing to turn

to good use, but the *who* of who you are can't be released without surrender to him, *Dod*, even if his makeup has elements
of the worst and is your only way of understanding half of
yourself—more in a male, more if you're bonded and tethered
as some daughters are (*I hate his guts!*), with your trade that pays
the way a heritage from him, apparent in your tools and toys
and texts, including computers—mechanical syntheses of cir-
cuits in the brain—since my best resource on the days when my
best lines arrive with both hands full (as I've learned) is a sound
mind, as when Aleksandr Solzhenitsyn composed *A Day in the
Life* by setting it sentence by sentence in memory, now and
then scratching with a piece of charcoal on toilet paper a phrase
he needed to *see*, then eating the toilet paper, so his guards
wouldn't know he was busy at the act that transported him from
his ragged prison walls, and once free of the Gulag he wrote the
novel from first sentence to last, aglow in its concentrated mass,
in the way Einstein as a child pictured masses of light bending
through time and spent the rest of his life (after early wordless
years) searching for a way to describe what he saw—scientists
and artists working with suppositions that arrive in rhythms
or images scratched across the consciousness, then a page, no
complaints about the speed of a computer when busy at that,
although in the looping scan my mind takes to return to an
earlier thought as in an echo, I admit creative minds might feel
the generating source of the impulse that works its way into
words, once the words are down, is out of fashion, unoriginal,
not quite right, and pause in untranslatable contretemps, as I
do this night under the secret descent of the essence Aleksandr
Solzhenitsyn and Joseph Brodsky carried in Siberia over their
shoulders, snow.

. . .

I wake with a leg uncovered, half of the fork of a biped dead cold, so unhinged by the night I feel suspended in the kind of hangover I had when I drank, the coils of my brain so soaked with poison all I could think was *Gag.*

Out the door snow is piled so deep the day is soundless, and it takes a quarter hour to clear it from the car. The plowed highway past the parking lot shines like tin in sun—ice beneath snow that began as rain—with fifteen hundred miles to go, nineteen done, packed the way we are. The rear bumper is cuddled in the cup of a drift, no shovel in the trunk, no room, so no opening night of the conference.

In the car I've had running to warm up, your mother says, "Your seat belt."

I seldom use it, as you know, and not in dunderheaded rebellion. When I started to drive, cars weren't equipped with belts or AC, power steering was a luxury, and in all but the newest models you had to use arm signals to show your intention to turn. So I seldom buckle up unless it's for a long trip.

Thirty miles and we're in South Dakota, where summery sun sears the ice to watery sheets, although drifted snow in spots sets off a wallowing roar I can feel in my feet through the floorboards, the weighty slush tugging at the wheel, and after a mile of this I release a long sigh.

"Do you want me to drive?" Care asks, a question almost a joke between us, but under a sensitive skin—that I would give up the wheel! When I drive I enter my driving mode and *drive,* unflagging, unfazed, unreachable, with no breaks for sleep (unless others insist) to my goal, the terminus. In that mode I drive no matter where I'm sitting so it's best, in terms of safety, to have me at the wheel, my mind fixed on a dot on the map, until I pull with a gentle braking to the end of a crackling drive, on time.

Her driving, as I find I have to mention, is erratic, daring or too cautious, a balance to mine. But when the daylight starts to wane I let her take the wheel. We may still make the opening night at this rate, although I'm not scheduled to speak until two evenings later, with workshops wedged between. Then on to the hacienda-style house in Arizona where Care's mother, widow for three years, presides. After your mother's last visit of aid, from July to November, I drove down in our pickup, with no AC, to ferry her back, and this is the next installment, with taxes to do and a book to finish, not knowing how long Grandma Peterson will want us to stay.

Last fall, in order to respond to my editor's suggestions when we were in Arizona, I bought a laptop, a used one off the Internet, and I take it from its canvas case and set it between the Lincoln hump and my knee and plug its power cord into an inverter connected to the cigarette-lighter socket or, in present parlance, since smoking is passé, the power point.

"Can you work like that?" Care asks.

"As long as I can type."

When I lay in bed the night before, sleepless, I decided not to do the talk I planned, so I turn to the one I've been fielding sentences for, Tolstoy as artist of spiritual space—his concept of space occurring (based on *Confession*) in a horrid limited packet of interior dark, and like any idea it seems grand until it begins its march onto a page.

Trust your intuition, Maxwell used to say, not that I was a clerical tabulator of a planned mode or accountant of the tricks of prosody, but he once said that when he met me he felt he'd stepped into a "Faustian struggle between the writer and the intellectual"—the idea of my being an intellectual so alien it raised hackles on my neck, when for me the conflict lay in saying exactly what I wanted to say with language that sounded exactly as I felt it should, the two becoming inseparable in my internal geography. Or maybe that was the conflict Maxwell meant after all. "Don't imagine you're not an intellectual," an analyst I saw in New York after my disassociated loss of identity, William Triebel, said. "You *think*. Most of the time too much."

To me intellectual then meant a crabbed Apollonian ambush of a limited subject confined inside an academy.

My control over a page was so strict I had to step past words to the unfolding imagery of the story, or dream my way into another consciousness, from the look on a face or the swivel of the head of a woman at a cocktail party—any visual clue set in motion the unreeling of a story as if on film. But the movement of words toward a page, in a clumsy tumble like airport luggage, dimmed the imagery, and I had to sort sounds from a lobby where a bamboozled crowd of shoppers kept rattling wrappings and paper bags—to speak metaphorically.

Which is to say dream-bound intuition was my mainstay, convoluted as it might be, but as much a dread as an aid, because I felt invaded by an alien upstart— *What was that?*—as accelerated rhythms overtook my hearing or I woke to the voice of a person I didn't know engaged in conversation with a person as unfamiliar, as if I were under siege. I numbed myself with alcohol once I was free of my daily pages. And anybody who has put down prose under the tilt of one too many knows how that extraordinary paragraph of late last evening has the appearance, in morning light, of mink fudge.

So I came to view "inspiration" with mistrust. But hardly an hour has passed since my grandmother put her hand on my head when I wasn't working with language or pawing through it with the aversion or grief of a lost soul rummaging through the closet of a relative recently dead (an image that becomes a pair of hands spreading typewriter keys banged with a fist, hopelessly stuck), searching for a word to fit a phrase or fill the connection between several to satisfy a sense of completion and bring a paragraph to its end.

So I learned you have to trust in the organic nature and structure of the story or novel, as all good editors do, or you shear away its potential to be original.

"What?" I ask, through phlegm, groggy from thought that grips me as in a petit mal seizure, so that rising from it I find my mouth open and slack and a tingling in my tongue and hands, in an aura of inhaling ozone after a lightning strike, a near miss. "What did you say?"

"The road's awfully icy again. Maybe you should drive."

The speedometer shows she's traveling thirty-five, and I realize, glancing at the weight over my thighs, that they're supporting a laptop I haven't been typing on.

"Do you have to drive so slow?"

"See for yourself," she says, and eases onto the shoulder in a slalom of braking.

I have to drive as slow to remain on the road, slick with ice. What happened to the South Dakota sun? Thoughts of Tolstoy arrive, now that I'm at the wheel and the laptop is in its bag, and the tedium of piloting the car at a horse's pace fades as I think of how, if there's a lesson to learn from Tolstoy it's never to disclose to a spouse your sexual past, as Lev the philanderer did when his wife begged for his diary.

Their marriage was never the same after that.

In a similar sense, you relent or choose what to reveal to your intimate, the reader (usually only one, *you*), or slyly suggest it—and meanwhile keep my eyes on the yellow line stuttering under ice outside the windshield before my thoughts congeal in inner blindness, though I do take in the road and its condition for now, just must keep thought on a leash so it doesn't hurtle off into a blotting of landscape and time and space, the struggle back and forth one of the wires a writer must tread.

When I consider the intensity of last night's blizzard and this residue of sun-enameled ice, I can see how somebody might imagine I cherish adventure or foolish challenge (yes, we still have the wood-burning furnace, for those who ask), but I don't set conference dates or regulate the weather and I don't angle after material for a book. I have enough to last two lifetimes. And I'm not a rebel. Or I certainly wasn't early on, and not because my father was hovering close, or so I can say now. I did not drink, not even a beer, in high school (except for one wine-soaked night), but did taste the air a rebel does, riding in aimless loops late at night with my friend John Paul, singing with the radio turned up high to the Big Bopper doing "Chantilly Lace" or the "*Eee!* Eee! Ooo, wah-wah!" of "The Witch Doctor," tattling in a giggling way about our not-quite conquests and smoking Lucky Strikes.

Work is an affront to the rebel, and writing, from the first, aroused in me an agitated fondness. I tried to reproduce the rhythms of poems I read and had the results printed in a local newspaper. Now, after decades of poems and stories and books, I've reached the age termed "senior"—a desolate desert of regret, as twenty-somethings view it, imagining the old guy's orange feet throbbing as badly in sandals as the vein under his white hair about to spray into Florida sky. We may be on our way to Arizona (to aid somebody older) but not on a last-ditch pilgrimage to that tribulus Mecca of sun-baked cacti sprouting spiky hairs of the sort you see on the old guy's big toe if you get close enough to the squalid state of dry moans age brings on. Or so youth imagines it, or I did. I'm the person I discovered in my interior the day I woke to the world, and I have to pause in surprise at reflections in glass that suggest the one gliding by isn't nineteen, feeling a sudden surge below where the bees of desire swarm and suck.

"Larry." This is a warning.

"I know. I'm tired." It's hardly four but almost dark. "Do you want to stop?"

"I thought you wanted to be there for the first night."

"It isn't as important as getting there in one piece. Do you want to stop?"

"If you do."

I'm about ready to contest this agreeable ambiguity when Laurel cries from her cramped backseat slot, "I do!"

We're three-quarters of the way down Nebraska, a pathetic day of a few hundred miles, but I'm weary from the weather and the tug-of-war of thought, as if I'm approaching an ambush. So I pull off at a motel and check us in and step into a room twinkling in speckled dimness, as if viewed through window screen, from the effects of driving on sun-glazed ice.

Laurel looks blue. If spiraling thought is the worst I encounter in the spells of disruption writing can cause, and I'm able to let others watch as I claw my way out, conscious of the possible shame in finding, or not, the right phrase, and can persevere in that, fine. Nobody can coax anybody down that route or, worse, set you on a course they expect you to take, as teachers and mentors, even the best, such as Maxwell, do. So I've adopted aloofness to your desire or reluctance to write, Joseph.

All of you have a gift for it, as Laurel does, stretching her legs in comfort, but the most I'll say, as I do to students and inquiring others, "Don't attempt to be a writer unless you feel called." It eats up years with little to show and has no patience with the rebel or slugabed rising with empty eyes from a wallow of covers at noon. You enter in submission and move ahead with minor jerks and sighs at its strictures and rules, because to rebel against the armies of the laws of language is futile, and if some do they don't last long, and even more die, as Saul Bellow has said, of heartbreak—biding time for a book never done.

I pull off my clothes and crawl into the closest bed and drop into the sleep that's eluded me for nights.

The snowplows and salt-and-sanding trucks have passed in the night, as we note at dawn, off early, still perhaps able to attend the first night's doings. The morning sun works on the ice and after an easy hundred miles I decide to let your mother drive, so I can tap more words into my laptop. I decide to make the switch outside the town of Geneva, for its associative context: Switzerland, Nabokov, chocolate, Calvin, army knife, Alps—refuge of writers for centuries.

A cold wind has picked up, as I catch full face when I step out to change seats, along with a peppering of grainy snow, but the road looks fine. I plug in my laptop and start typing a paragraph I composed as I drove, the words falling in place, and in a pause think, *Oh, all right,* and pull my seatbelt around underneath the laptop, and buckle up.

At that moment your mother says, "I'm afraid the road is getting icy again."

"Don't worry. We don't have to be there tonight."

We glance at each other and I nod, suspended in the thought

arriving through my fingertips, relieved, distracted, and then, a quarter mile off, I see a pickup clear the crest of a hill and, as if struck by a gale broadside, slide off into the angle of a sideways skid.

"Carole, that pickup is out of control."

"I know, I see, I can't brake."

I realize that the black beneath us isn't blacktop but black ice, a sudden shadowed plateau of it.

The pickup, a dark shape, starts to swing the other way and in a slow correction comes back around but at an angle aimed at us and I want to yell, "Go for the ditch!" but the pickup, which at first seemed the size of a toy, has gained the bulk of an actual pickup, a Mack truck, a cataract wide as the windshield, and a report like a load of tin plates dynamited arrives with the airy nasal blue blaze of unconsciousness.

It's not much later when, bound in a choking neck brace, in a wasteland of white, I find I'm being trundled on a gurney along a line of white ambulance vans, exactly as it was delivered to me in the fluttery black-and-white film two days ago—a warning I wouldn't heed but that you, in your concern for others you've inherited from your mother, dear son, would have taken gladly as a reason to settle into a week of winter solace and silent nights.

II

SWING POINTS

8

Father as Child

———

In a jump yet one step back, which might seem an entry to the future, I hear you knock snow off your shoes outside the door, and when you step into the house I see you have on your gray uniform slacks and dark rayon jacket and service belt, the elastic waistband of the jacket bulging over a pistol at your hip, a case of shiny handcuffs centered at your back.

"Hi, Mom," you say, and go to the sink and kiss her on the cheek and step back, ruddy from the cold, and the miniature room appears to contract as you smile down from your height and twirl your cop cap, removed when you entered, on a fingertip.

"I wear a beeper two or three days a week now"—you tap your other hip—"and have to be in town if a call comes in."

This seems an explanation for not living here while we're

away, but in your rented house in town, alone, and though we don't know how long we'll be in Arizona, you've promised to keep the wood-burning furnace stoked while we're away. You have enough daylight hours when you're on duty, you've said, "and of course on my days off," to keep it going, and when I suggest again that you stay at the farm, to conserve on travel, you say, "Oh, no!" in a deferential tone that reminds me of my younger brother, Chuck. You remind me of him so often that sometimes, in my absence from the present to acknowledge that and then my swim back up from the past, I call you Chuck.

You are a county deputy sheriff, recently licensed for CPR, and so you tap the beeper again. You pilot the ambulance to its gory sites and once told me it took four of you (first stuffing your nostrils with Vicks) to carry a fragile man from an apartment where he had been decomposing for a week. Plus the high school car wrecks, a few each fall.

We stand in such proximity I take in the scent of your aftershave and remember the six of us squeezing past one another in this kitchen so small your mother deplored it, in the years we grew up together, as it seems—your mother and I our ways, the four of you into adults, and now you stand above us like a stranger, your impetus to aid and protect and shelter others your inheritance from both of us, perhaps.

You were in diapers when we arrived, Newlyn ten, Ruth and Laurel born in our back bedroom, through the dining room from the kitchen where we mill. I attended all four births, the last two alone (signing the birth certificates "Dr. Woiwode" in honor of an honorary degree), and it seems I transport Laurel straight from my catch of her to the crib we had to line with books before she would sleep, and from there she's the tall and athletic scholar in our midst, the one who helps with fencing

and fixing as you and Ruth once did. She smiles, pleased at your
company, you two more allied than Newlyn and Ruth, another
complementary pair, though they might disagree on that, since
their similarities arouse tension; sturdy blondes who love to
train horses, and are artistic, skillful at any handiwork, passion-
ate in their views, and animated storytellers besides.

I tend to pace at the thought of how the four of you have
traveled from us at a rate that seems akin to light, while time
keeps constant but propels your mother and me backward,
and I remember Maxwell saying to me after Newlyn was born,
"Soon she'll be a teenager and you'll be an old man"—one of the
times he laughed so hard it seemed he wouldn't stop.

I look forward to seeing you not because you're our son but
the adult I prefer to talk to and work with, after saddling you
with the expectations laid on any only son, and, once Newlyn
was married, the added yoke of the oldest—that grief-laden
responsibility of keeping a family true to its lights—and protec-
tor of your sisters. I think of you when I see a child of intellectual gravity stare at a playful parent, the kind given to frivolity
and joking, with the solemnity of sorrow, as I'm sure you stared
more than once at me.

Earlier this year, during another of your mother's trips to
Arizona to tend to *her* mother, you stopped by in uniform,
embraced me in greeting, stepped out onto the stairs where
I'll stand five years later on that cold August morning when I
decide to go in for a jacket, beckoning me after, and then closed
the door with its clump of sound, and said in the cold, out of
earshot of Laurel, "Are you drinking again?"

"Not really. The night you saw me." A week before, on duty
as the town cop, by way of the sheriff's office, you came through
a bar on your beat and saw me at a table with the kind of crowd

bars are built on, finishing my first hard drink in a year. For seven years I kept to the internal promise at your hospital bed not to drink, not one, not even during a semester in London, when I passed a pub on nearly every block for six months. But after seven years I told your mother it was time for a sabbatical and drank now and then, not often, but a few times in a troubling way, so again I said I would stop.

"Sometimes I go to one of the bars for a six-pack of Coke when nothing else is open," I say to you. "Really."

"Is that what you had in the bag the night I saw you to the car, when you'd had a whiskey, or whatever?"

I look down, suffering an inner quaking at the intensity of your stare, and know this is a time I can't lie—not only because I've vowed not to, for the damage dishonesty does to prose, but because it's you. "No," I say.

It was a six-pack, I think, unable to speak the words.

Plumes of vapor stream from your nose as you sigh in the cold, but you refrain from saying what I suspect has been on your mind since my time as a tenured professor in the East: *Isn't it time you learned?*

We survived the impact with the pickup, or these hands wouldn't work, but a patrolman who filed a report on the accident said, "If you hadn't been in that heavy Lincoln and had your seat belts on, besides the ice allowing for a lot of give when you connected"—spinning our car 180 degrees to face the opposite direction—"I wouldn't be talking to you."

He doubted either of us was traveling faster than forty, yet the battery behind the Lincoln's grill was wedged against the firewall, visible past the jackknifed hood from the head-on not quite dead center, the passenger half caved worse, a clutter

of smashed plastic trim and debris scattered a hundred yards
across the ditch and into a neighboring field, skidding that far
on icy snow at the explosive impact.

"Get out!" I yelled, once I was conscious, imagining us going
up in flames. I heard groans from somewhere and cried, "Are
you OK?"—meaning alive. I was levered so tight against the
dash I could barely move and saw blood over the steering wheel
and felt it running down one eye. My door was jammed from
the leverage of connection. "Out!"

Your mother got her door open and pushed past the bent
steering wheel, holding her nose, torn loose along one side, and
I was gasping for breath and groaning over a thumb I could feel
to my elbow. The second I knew we would collide I started closing the laptop, my left thumb under the lid as it connected with
the dash and my solar plexus. Laurel thought I was dying, my
head back, color gone (she told me), gagging for breath. Once
we were out the driver's door, I had to comfort her in the sleet-
ing cold as Care fell to her hands and knees and cupped snow
over her bleeding face in a melt of crimson into white.

I heard a semi and saw its stack behind the hill where the
pickup went awry and pictured it taking a sideways skid, wiping the two-lane road clean of us and the car, and started to
say we had to run, but somebody had stopped at the sight of
the accident and ran up the road to flag down the semi as it
rose over the hill's crest. Laurel's hips and head hurt and it was
the weight of the boxes on the driver's side that hurtled your
mother with such damaging force into the steering wheel.

I staggered to the pickup, partly on the shoulder ahead, actually behind our spun car, sitting at a tipped angle, with a man at
the wheel and a woman across from him. They could talk but he
was incoherent, puzzled about where he was, a pair of webbed

bulges in the windshield where their heads had struck—sister and brother, we learned at the hospital where the ambulance vans ferried us all. Her ribs were broken, a pain I need not imagine, but one of hers had pierced a lung, and soon she was airlifted by helicopter to Lincoln. I swayed at the driver's door of the pickup, saw her crouched against the passenger window, a hand to her chest, barely able to speak, but heard her whisper, "I'm so sorry. We slid. Forgive us."

I think it was then I decided to pray.

My head was cut, my thumb sprung so painfully I couldn't use it for a year, a knee banged so badly pain poured through my back teeth. Laurel's hips were bruised, with a raised welt across the front edge from a rear seat belt with no shoulder strap, but Care was cruelly hurt. The plastic surgeon who re-attached her nose said he had never seen one quite so bad, and had to stitch part of it in place from the inside. But once that was done she wouldn't stay in the hospital. Our X-rays showed no further injuries, so we checked in at a motel and lay groaning on a pair of beds.

A wrecker towed our car to a garage a block away and I hobbled to a service station the motel owner mentioned and rented a van, then limped back and forth between the van and the car, reloading everything I once loaded in snowfall. Both your mother's eyes were black by morning, but she wanted to leave. We made it to the conference the afternoon of the evening I was scheduled to speak. My laptop was shattered, not a word in it usable, so I read from the proofs of the memoir that would appear in the spring, and talked between passages about the border between autobiography and fiction, when there is one.

Updike has said that when you use characters unlike yourself "you have to conceive them in the round. Your own self is kind of boundary-less . . . You don't really know what you're like. And so often things written out of the center of your experience are weaker than something written out of the margins. And that kind of reaching into the margins is something Bill [Maxwell] did then, in *Time Will Darken It.*"

The novel was the first Maxwell wrote when he parted from the *New Yorker* in the 1940s, hoping to make a go of writing, and he told me that after it appeared, when he was busy in his workroom with the door closed, a cubicle in the modest country house the Maxwells moved to at that time, he would hear his wife Emily go for the mail to their rural mailbox. "Then I'd hear Em's steps come up the porch, past my workroom, through the living room and kitchen and out the back door, and I'd hear the clang of the garbage-can lid. More lousy reviews."

The next year he returned to the magazine.

I conducted the workshops, gripping my thumb to compress the pain, and Laurel and your mother didn't leave the motel once they settled in. Earlier, when she walked into a grocery store a woman hurried up and asked if she was OK, seeing her blackened eyes, as if she'd suffered spousal abuse, and that was enough. The surgeon did such wonderful work, however, her nose healed with only a hairline scar, now invisible.

Most farmers and ranchers are missing a finger or carry scars or work with mended limbs, and in *The Fear of Flying*, a novel by a 1970s poet who became a novelist, Erica Jong, her central character suggests we can chart our personal histories by the scars on our body, so I present some of mine, in this, and in every sentence I carry to the unmarred surface of a page, where the best of them adhere or hold as we would like those we love to hold on, unchanging in affection, through eternity.

And every sentence is a question of who I am over its course, an assemblage of words sorting out my consciousness at the moment, recording a newly forming identity, just as every act we undertake proves or disproves who we think we are. The faults in my sentences, or my scars, then, might be the only truthful record I carry into the future.

I won't presume to imagine the state of the pair in the pickup (we heard from the sister later, in apology), but I know the fascination of Americans for cars and the mythic sense cars assume in our culture. A vehicle may be our love, perhaps our only one when we're single, cruising alone through the night, but also serves as a sounding board for the worst in us, when we honk or jam the brakes or go squalling off, and a car can become a flying wedge or battering ram, a portable dungeon for the cheapest rapist, the enforcer we end up wrapping around our bodies, because any moment in the best vehicle has the potential to bring death in a dark ditch. My fondness for our boat-like Lincoln and pride in my ability to fill its trunk in a writerly way fogged my good sense and endangered our lives, especially your mother's, I confess.

Instruction is meant to prepare us for what may come, but few instructors will admit that every forward inclination, even a life-enhancing one, is another step toward death. And if you feel I keep stepping further from the present, yes, I do. The past is my secure sector of existence—everything I've been through, no matter how trying it may have been, is over. It's death that lies ahead, through the membrane of the future, unless that membrane arrives in a flying embrace when I reenter the secure harbor the past once was and dally there too long.

On a sunny afternoon Maxwell says to me as we sit in his office, "A reviewer once said about a book of mine, 'All he writes about is childbirth and death,' and I thought, How can he say that? Then I thought, But what could be more important? One or the other is the beginning or end of nearly every story, often with more of the same in between."

Death is our destiny, of course, and one either accepts that at the age I've reached or, as youth will do, pretend it doesn't exist. Leon Edel said that the essence of Willa Cather's writing was "conquest and death," the same idea, really, if birth is viewed as a kind of conquest, as it is. The book of hers that seems the most dangerous to her personal equilibrium, is *The Professor's House*, though *My Mortal Enemy* comes close, and the one that records the receding Dakota life we've shared is *O Pioneers!*

So here is how you grow up, Joseph. First you're the boy who follows me, then the one I can't do without, and then every attribute is wiped away in the accident that leaves you in a coma for a week. You rise from it not yourself. In the weeks before we head East, I take you fencing, as I said, and then set in front of you the rocks you collected over our summer vacation to the Southwest, a scavenging you and Laurel have taken up, and insist that you identify each one and arrange them in a display. I find the names of most using an encyclopedia and a *Guide to Rocks*.

Then I help you out to my office and seat you at my Selectric, the technology of the day, and guide you through the typing of each identifying tag, one letter at a time.

"No, you know what an R is," I say, and will not let up. You're hardly able to walk or speak, and look up with the pleading eyes of the dog your mother was concerned you would imitate too well, but I say, not about to relent, "Yes, you must get this done."

My sense is that if you use your hands, so adept, they will engage higher echelons in a healing rearrangement, as when I got down on the floor with you and crawled. I refuse to let up. I won't give way until you have each name typed and the spelling correct. You aren't able to use scissors, so I cut the names into strips but insist that you glue each rock in place, on a slab of plywood with a frame, no matter how difficult, your hands quaking and jerking away from the pressure to do this right. And then I make you paste the labels, a more difficult task, beneath each rock, and they remain to this day at their varying angles.

Your mother helps you relearn speech, which you begin to use with greater ease but without your gift of wit and wry riposte. You're stiff on your legs, off kilter, as if your center of balance has undergone a change—before this so agile and fluid in your engaging grace, and I follow every move with grief for the Joseph you were. I'll never write about this, I tell myself, I can't, and resting in counterbalance to that are the stories and books and essays and poems I mean to write, routes I might take, but none of that, not a bit of it matters now, with the direction of your life in our hands and you not yourself.

I hold you in my lap as my father held my sisters beyond the age I thought they should be held, because I could remember the heat he gave off when I sat as they did with his arm around me after our mother died, and know the comfort it must have been to them and how we are able to comfort others only with the comfort that comforts us. Anything else is alien. The best remedy for the ills of a child and anybody else, too, as far as I know, is the outpouring of attention we commonly call (often with an uneasy sense of emptiness) love.

It would take another book to cover the child in me as father, so I'll examine my father from another angle, an easy out. Besides his job as teacher and administrator, he was a layer-on of plaster undercoat in summer, a laborer, and as well-read as anybody I knew before I went to college. He kept up on current novels through the Book of the Month club but returned to favorite passages in Hugo or Dickens or Poe. He read the newspaper every evening while he smoked a cigar, read a dozen histories a year, and began to appreciate biographies.

It may have been this interest that set off the idea of a history of his life. He was a diarist, and the beginning of his quest probably came late one night as he sat under the lamp at his fold-down desk, the time of day when he corresponded with friends, his pipe in his mouth, bowl smoking. He started jotting down notes, and then began listing chapter titles.

Work that my father began, such as remodeling our house, took too long or remained unfinished, a trait that I, if no others, have inherited. Late in his life he had forty chapter titles listed and ten of them finished, besides other pieces he had written and had on hand. One begins, "November 16, 1967, I picked up a snap that was fastened to a loop to be worn on my belt," and I feel my hair crawl, due to its similarity to the opening of a story your mother began in the same tight-tied rhythm, like the object he's describing. It's the belt loop to which he clipped his school keys, beginning with our years in North Dakota, and he describes his concern about their location, first with my mother: "'Audrey, where are my keys?' was a usual cry years ago as my mind was really on the problems that might face me as I walked into the brick building which prominently displayed . . .

"'Well, where did you put them last night before you went out to the farm?'"

This was the farm of a friend he worked on from the spring through the fall, drawn by the scent of turned earth. He says my mother was "engrossed in getting breakfast, quieting young-sters, while in her mind she was trying to organize a full day as a housekeeper"—before the word was outré. "Then came the ten years after her death when the children would scramble" to get the keys to him "before too many threats." I don't remember any scramble or threats about his keys. Maybe I was asleep.

He writes of how "a beautiful woman came along who was largely preoccupied with an ailment that was given many names in hopes that it did not turn out to be what it really was—malignant cancer"—his second wife, Lorraine. And when in the morning he is "quietly picking up the keys (by now one had learned to place them down quietly in the evening) it was an opportune time to ask, 'How did you rest last night, Lorraine?'

"So that November day in 1967 [after Lorraine had died of cancer] when the keys were in place the first reaction was, 'Now everything is as it used to be.' How wrong! Where are you, Audrey? Where are the children? Lorraine, did you rest well last night?

"Keys only remind you of the past—they must now be used in a present that will some day mislay them."

The last sentence seems to foretell his death, soon to come, as the fluttery film was a preview and warning of mine.

The year the horse injured you was your worst, Joseph, as seen from the outside. We took the advice of a friend, the poet Milt Kessler (whose sister-in-law was aided after a near-fatal accident), and had you examined at the NYU Institute of Physiatry, a new specialty. Their battery of tests left them skeptical about your recovery, like the previous doctors, but they prescribed exercises to improve hand-eye coordination and aid inner connections. Soccer was your favorite sport, but you could barely kick the ball, and once when I was at work and you were practicing on our concrete drive you spun around and hit the cement so hard (your mother said) you tore the skin off a kneecap, an awful injury to see. It hardly fazed you. You swung from dull disinterest to too much activity, and would run off from us as if to escape the state imprisoning you, or its jailers. I felt as responsible as my father did for my mother's death.

The next year I took a leave of absence, moved by your entreaties to stay on the farm. I was tenured but wanted time to weigh the wisdom of returning—due to you, yes, and your younger sisters' chorus in the same key. But more than once at the university, in my amiable situation, I ran into roadblocks. Chauvinism and outright racism and prejudice were absent from its halls, a welcome habitat, but undergraduates who held traditional religious or spiritual or, especially, Christian views were targets to some professors. Students came to me and complained of how they were cut off before they could finish an opinion or ridiculed by a professor. A number of them said they came to study with me and I began to feel I was attracting a certain student who was, to the academy's gods—that line from *Lear*—as flies to wanton boys; to swat for the sport.

When a thirty-year-old grad student came to my office in tears because she brought up a point in a class on Puritan literature and was subjected to such public verbal abuse by the instructor she had to leave, I went to the department chair. He was sympathetic, he listened with attention as I told him about this and previous incidents, and then he said—as the principal of the public school Newlyn was required to attend said to her when she turned to him while a boy in the line for the bus kept beating her on her back and she asked him to do something about it—"What is it you expect me to do?"

Now I'll tell the worst of it, Joseph. The summer after my leave, when I decided not to return, was a time of distraction and remorse, due partly to you, though you were improving, advancing, and the doctor who prescribed your exercises said to your mother when we brought you in for a follow-up battery of tests, "I don't know what it is you're doing, but whatever it is, keep it up. This is amazing."

But during the summer it comes to me that I'll never hold quite such a congenial job, one that pays so well, and only a year from my first sabbatical. I have a book out, *Born Brothers,* my best, I believe (yes, writers tend to think the latest is their best, but a case could be made for this one), that is receiving tepid or obtuse reviews or, as with the cover review it shared in the *Times Book Review,* a bit of both.

I'm also sunk in self-pity, due to the above, and summer is

the season when my work never goes well, although it's a lovely day, or so I see out the raised door of the garage where I sit in shadow on a nail keg. I'm thinking of my father in his last years, when he oversaw houses and apartments for elderly widows in the city where he lived, and in the basement of each set up a work bench with a stool beside it or cleared a space and moved in a chair, as he had in his garage, next to a potbellied stove, and sat in silence for hours at a time, staring ahead. *When men sit that way,* I thought, *with that look, they are old indeed.*

Out the door I watch you race across the lawn on a riding mower we bought from the Berns a decade ago, so dilapidated and in need of repair I had to help you get it started. The latest problem is its mowing platform, which has a tendency to slip from one of two hooks that hold it level, usually after a bump, and I've been intending to repair it, because once the platform comes unhooked on the left and falls, digging into the ground on that side, you have to shut off the engine, wait for the whistling blades to stop, and then drag the platform forward while lifting it, in order to reattach the hookup.

I stare over the sun-streaked landscape and think through the mechanical steps it will take to complete the repair when the tractor goes dead at a far corner of the lawn, beside the raised drive, and I see you rise from beside it.

"Dad!" you scream. *"Dad! Dad!"*

And I know what's happened—in your state, your mind elsewhere, you went to reattach the platform without shutting the mower off. In moments of crisis I'm jolted into the detached precision of an emergency room physician, but when I see the fingers, third and fourth, of your left hand—I'm at your side, gripping your wrist, as if I've flown there—I give way. Torn pieces dangle from skin, blood pumping out with your heart-beats, shattered so badly that only a father, as I've heard in your cry, can fix this.

Then we're inside, at a sink where I try to rinse things clean. I wrap your hand with a washcloth to staunch the blood, and so I don't have to see it. Your mother is attending an opera in a city across the state, so we roar off in the car, but when you seem faint I stop on the way and have a friend drive us on to Bismarck, so I can sit in the backseat and hold you. "It doesn't hurt so bad now, Dad. Thanks."

At the hospital, while you're being X-rayed, I get on the phone to a doctor so skilled in micro-surgery he's often flown to St. Paul for severe cases, and he says, "I'm just out of surgery myself. Hemorrhoids! I can't sit or walk, I can hardly think! I'll send in a good guy."

The doctor he recommends puts you on intravenous anti-biotics, and whisks you into the operating room of the same hospital you were in after the accident with the horse. During the wait for you to wake from anesthesia, I sit at the foot of your bed and start a story I've had in mind for a year, the days of your coma too close to contemplate.

"Dad?" you say, as if you're unsure, and the story stops. You stare at your swaddled hand. "Will it be OK?"

"Fine, the doctor said. Better than he thought. He says chil-dren who are growing keep producing new cells, so it looks better for you than it would, say, for me."

"I shut the mower off but the blades must have still been spinning. I was in a hurry."

You're home the next day, with pins in two fingers, grieved at your stupidity, as you call it. But you were fixing the mower

on your own, as you often did, an ingrained reflex, with only
that thought: *fix*. I think of your brash and rowdy assertiveness
before the other accident, an attitude that came when we least
expected it, illogical, unguarded, goofy, and was seen by others
as mischief but was camouflage for your sensitivity, as with
Hemingway, one of the most sensitive males to assemble a body
of autobiographical fiction.

I've endured my share of mishaps and most I'm able to send
to the recycle bin, but when that moment returns, of you at
your entry into adolescence, holding up a hand and crying *Dad!*
Dad! I want to claw up a wall and keep on over the ceiling or
whatever it takes to escape my helplessness to undo the past.

I can't stop a pickup from sliding into us on ice or a thousand-
pound horse on a headstrong tear, but there's no way I can
escape this—not seeing to your safety as a father should.

And you who philosophize (as in a Dylan song) and believe
that we're accident prone, you citizens of appointed offices who
ride the subway home, you who at your seminars adopt a superior tone, take the hanky away from your face; the laborers and
cops who keep you safe, the farmers who feed you food each
day, putting in hours beyond their fears, the maids and laborers
from day to day face dangers you can scarcely imagine, on
cranes and scaffolds and country gravel, on ladders and swing
shifts and diesel gangs, deep in the ground and five miles up,
soldiers at sea or in desert dunes, so take the veil away from
your face.

All you have to do is walk home.

9

In Community

———

So, Joseph, it's time to unite this to the community of its first volume, where I mention my beginnings in this craft or sullen what-you-may-call-it, and I'll pick up where that one left off, with *What I'm Going to Do, I Think* taken by a publisher, and do a quick run. Before Care and I leave New York with three-month Newlyn to live with Dad, as we decide to do, I correct the manuscript of my first novel and sell a second, *Beyond the Bedroom Wall,* to the same house, and they want to meet with me before I take off for good.

First your mother and I drive to Illinois pulling a trailer filled with manuscripts and breakables to Dad's house (more later), and though he has Ms. Jong's fear of flying he flies back with me, saying, "Maybe they'll let me carry a box of dirt inside the plane to put my feet in. That's what Smokey Stover"—a cartoon character, a precursor to the Cat in the Hat—"does. He carries a box of dirt along so he can keep his feet on the ground."

From the airport we take a cab to Brooklyn Heights and when it stops I look past his profile at the pin oak in front of our entry door with longing. "Your building," he says. I get on my bike, a ten-speed your mother got for my first Father's Day, and ride it to a garage on Fulton Street, where I've reserved a U-Haul truck. It's not there.

The wait extends until I have to rent a car to get to my appointments—lunch with my publishers, dinner with Candida, my agent—and I toss the bike in the trunk and rush back to get Dad and race back to the rental place, feeling him apply imaginary brakes all the way, and pick up the truck that by now is waiting, and roar back with him following in the car and help him load furniture it takes two to carry, leaving stacks of boxes and cartons and furniture yet to go.

I get to Union Square so quick I can't remember Brooklyn Bridge (*How many dawns, chill from his rippling rest*), and Roger Straus and Bob Giroux and my editor, Michael di Capua, walk me to a Greek restaurant where the waiters pull towels from their arms and slap at our chairs before we sit. I tell the three I'm worried about the dust jacket for my novel, after the Martin Luther King and Robert Kennedy assassinations, both of which happened that spring, once the artwork was approved. I think we should pull it, I say.

Roger's hand goes up. "But you—"

Yes, I designed the jacket, constructing a collage from magazine cutouts before the novel was sold, when a picture of a rifle lying in grass arrived as I was finishing a final draft, visualizing its exact angle on the cover, and later told Roger how much I liked the artwork, done by Symeon Shimin. Shimin located the model of Winchester purchased by Chris, the protagonist, and was able to rent and carry it, no questions asked, into Central Park—a different era. He laid it in the grass, climbed up a tree, edged out on a limb overhanging the rifle, and sketched it at the angle in my collage, on a lozenge of grass framed by leaves. The set-aside rifle is the turning point in the novel, abandoned by Chris before he runs to his wife Katherine, and I was sure the iconography would attract bookstore buyers.

Roger's rug-like wavy hair slides in querying animation as he turns to Bob, then Michael, and he says nobody but a loony would make any connection between my cover and the loonies who do such things, not to worry, with a hint of his swagger in a blazer and ascot as he strode down a dingy hall at the offices of Farrar, Straus to the mail room and piled a dozen books in my arms; then took me to meet the director of book production, the "rights" people, the publicity director, the in-house proofreaders and copyeditors, and his son, Roger III, recently hired as head of marketing.

Bob says Roger likely is right and Michael, who seems to consider my reservations, says if the book is coming out this fall, that would be one thing, but by next spring, no. "I'm afraid the collective memory is that brief," he says.

"Anyhow," Roger says, "we're doing something special for you, baby, and, until this very moment, undisclosed, and your cover's already in production—right, Michael?"

Michael studies his hands, small but durable-looking, resting on the tablecloth. "I believe so."

"Already in production!" I exclaim.

Roger winks and says the reaction of first readers is so positive he's decided on a treat for me—print three hundred advance copies in trade paperback to stir up further interest. "We'll knock 'em dead with this book, baby!"

Which increases my uneasiness about the rifle, as I'm about to say, when Bob, leaning his portly rose-red face so close I can see squiggles of vessels in his cheeks, says, "About the second book, the children grow up, don't they?"

His accent is hard to place, perhaps suave New Jersey of a Princetonian cast, with his patrician poise that recalls Edmund Wilson and F. Scott Fitzgerald. He once asked the same question when we were meeting about the contract for my second book in a Longchamps restaurant where Miss Welty, as he called her, appeared. He introduced us that day, and now I tell him that in one chapter of that book, "the one Eudora Welty liked, two of the brothers are in college. In another, one's an intern."

"But seen in that light only at the story's end," Bob says. "Otherwise most of them remain, in the pieces I've read, adolescents or younger. We will see them mature."

This isn't a question, and he smiles, his teeth tight together in the genial glow of his rubicund face.

Oh, yes! I say, and not only that, I recently had a kind of vision about earlier generations, those before the parents of the children, and plan to include a section on them—as adults, of course. A scattering of looks passes among the three and Roger sits back. "Not *too* ambitious!" he says. "Not the second time around. That's when the bastards are itching to cut your balls off. Let's let 'em have both barrels with the first!"

"*What I'm Going to Do, I Think* is a beautiful title," Michael says. "It's a lovely book. And the pieces of the new one I've seen are even better."

. . .

From there I have to run to meet Candida, who has left a message with Michael that I should pick her up outside her building. It's on 57th Street, above the Steinway showroom where grand pianos straddle Turkish rugs, and when I pull up Candida isn't in sight. Rush hour is on and people spill over the curbs, skirting parked cars in their hurry. I figure Candida has given up. I circle the block in a creep and park in a yellow zone in front of the Steinway canopy and run inside and take an elevator up. Candida covers the mouthpiece of a phone she's on. "I was about to come down when this jerk from Hollywood called," she says. "Sit."

I like her no-nonsense style, the way she pulls her hair back for the primacy of business and masses it in a coiled bun, and the resonance of her throaty alto that edges toward baritone. She talks in street language, especially to resistant publishers, men, who "imagine they can get my writers on the cheap," and she once said to one with a reputation for stinginess, "Hey, are you getting so tight you carry your pee-pee home in a jar?"

When people ask who my agent is I say with a smile, "Candida Donadio," feeling the *D*s send a buzz through the tip of my tongue.

She hangs up and we hurry down to the canopy. The car is gone. No, it's being trundled behind a police tow truck toward Carnegie Hall. I take off on a run and when the truck stops for a light I wriggle past cars and knock on the passenger window. An officer in a baseball cap cranks the glass down an inch.

"That's my car!" I cry. "Where are you— Hey!"

The truck pulls off and horns honk on all sides.

Candida says fixing a situation like this is her métier, and hurries me upstairs to her office. On the phone she discovers it will take an hour, minimum, before the city can say which lot the car is impounded in. I call Dad to let him know, and there's no answer. I try again in a while and after a dozen rings picture the neighbors above and below turning to our empty apartment, and hang up.

Candida cancels our reservations at a restaurant now too far off, in an era of no cell phones, then draws open a drawer and sets a bottle of Scotch on her desktop. "I know a little restaurant, close, with a handy phone."

I drink too much, then and with the meal, in my worry over the car and no answer at Dad's end. Candida suspects he went for dinner; I know he wouldn't without me. I mention the uneasiness I felt from Roger and Bob during our lunch, and she says, "Michael will stick by you; he's a good guy"—in contrast to the bad guys? Or so I wonder.

By the time we learn the location of the lot and get the car out of hock for a fee I can't believe—Candida pulls fifties from her purse—it's 9:00 at night. I drive her to her apartment on East 19th and in a swiveling turn outside the car door she leans in and says, "Come up for coffee? You can use my phone."

She handles her writers with a familiarity and firmness outsiders call maternal, and keeps pictures of them and their children pinned to the office wall above her head. I notice other pictures in her apartment, plus trendy artifacts that suggest an occupant my age, though more austere. I mention something along those lines, and she says, "Kid," and I see her nostrils flare. She's called me Kid from the day we met (*The* Kid, actually, because, as I assumed, I was twenty-something), and now she says, "Kid, you know, I'm only a few years older. I got into the old lady look when I went into the business and was only nineteen."

She kicks off her heels, undoes the bun, shakes out her long dark hair, and in the dim light her features take on the shining

composure of youth, her almond eyes at a level below mine
with her shoes shed. One night she had one drink too many and
said her only memory as a child was sitting on or in a bathtub,
watching her father shave—

Feeling poured from her and she stopped, sat back, and
never continued, and I've wondered what she started to say.
Did her father misuse her devotion, or take advantage of her as
he shouldn't? She didn't trust men, so I felt, and I doubted she
ever met one she couldn't put in his place. But the men she got
involved with were young jerks and hucksters, versions of the
guys on her neighborhood street corner.

She grew up in the same neighborhood as Mario Puzo and
Bob, as she calls Robert Gottlieb, to whom she sent Joe (Joseph
Heller—besides Peter and Philip and John and Tom and Frank,
among dozens of others, mostly men, but also Sue and Hortense
and Edna and others), and my sense of her acumen with writers
of high caliber and cash value increases the specific gravity I've
perceived as age and sets her, weighty with portent, on this side
of the gulf I imagine exists between a young man and a woman
over thirty. Or so I imagine until I grow up.

No answer from Dad yet. Candida goes into a shallow
kitchen off the entry and puts on water for coffee. *In vino veri-
tas*, perhaps, although a step beyond that is the pit of deception,
sensory and otherwise, depicted in another proverb: "Wine is
a mocker and strong drink raging, and whoever is deceived
thereby is not wise." I sway and register her beauty bared at
every line by accomplishment and go weak at the sight. She's
talking about Roger, as if continuing our dinner conversation,
and how he perplexes her, one of those macho publishers she
doesn't get.

She seldom attends parties or receptions, she says, but went to one of the soirees at Roger's townhouse in the East 60s ("Wall-to-wall celebrities!" an editor from the *New Yorker* cried when he walked in on one) and made her way upstairs to Roger's bedroom, bare as a monk's cell, with a single bed like a cot, and tried to take in his aura, she says, to figure out why he slept here, when the rest of the house was so elegant—Roger of Old New York Family, the money behind Farrar, Straus, with family ties to the Moes and Guggenheims. So she's thrown by the way his debonair grace can switch, as I saw today, to the swagger and language of a pirate.

Her kitchen is white, a blare of white, with a white-and-black tile floor, and she revolves under an overhead fixture like a voluptuary from Titian painted by Vermeer. I see a white carpet in the living room, the couch and chairs white, and down a hall past the bathroom (from a peek on a pee run), a black-and-white rug beside her bed, which is covered with a white spread pulled as taut as the cloth of a banquet table—all emblematic of her calling, the words she must survey, black on white, right and wrong, good or bad.

The intuitive and nearly wordless way editors of the best rank work, entering a story as if slipping into a second skin, is her gift. There's no middle ground in the best of fine-tuned writing. It works or it doesn't, or it works except for this paragraph and the ending. Phrases and endings can be fixed, along with boundaries of gray, every wobbly sentence falling aside or, with work, turning solid, and that's her baby and why she's the top literary agent in the city.

From Dad I've learned to bow to providence, to depend on others, which is why I get along, as I do, with Maxwell and Michael and copyeditors and proofreaders and dust jacket

designers, *and with her,* I think—a newcomer to her beauty
with the power to disrupt. I take a step toward her and she raises
a hand without turning, and says, "No. Never."

I sink to the floor, because I find myself on the white carpet
as she tries to call Dad, seeing her feet, bare, petite, elegant,
toes crimping at my stare, and take one in my hands and try
to kiss it. When I wake in the same spot the phone is ringing.
She plucks the receiver and talks to somebody dear, from her
tone, and I point to my wristwatch—almost midnight—and
walk out.

It's the closest I came to ruining our relationship.

A new role I've assumed with Maxwell is cabaret clown or
jester, and when I run up to his office the next day and tell the
story about the mix-up the day before, I leave out the late night
with her. I tell him how, when Care and I were driving back, I
shifted into reverse at the wrong exit before I remembered the
trailer was behind and bent the bumper hitch so badly I had to
keep finding stones along the roadside to hammer it in place,
imagining the trailer taking the car and all of us on a mountainous tumble down the Delaware Water Gap, and then passing a
car in the median, with a U-Haul trailer identical to ours lying
on its side ahead of a tumultuous tumble of cartons and clothes,
as if my fears had taken substance; and how, when I rode my
bike down Fulton, bus drivers and cabbies kept trying to take
me out and then I realized the rental place was in Bedford-
Stuyvesant; the costly peril of renting a car to make the appointments, racing back to get the truck, and parking the truck in
a no parking zone I assured Dad was safe, and then returning
after 1:00 AM to find him asleep in the cab with a ticket on
the window. It was the only way to protect our belongings, he

decided, once the truck was loaded and ticketed, and that was why I couldn't reach him on the phone all night.

Maxwell laughs and says, "It sounds like a series of mishaps of the sort you can only rid yourself of by writing about." Which suggests another form of expression, since his rule of thumb has been you cannot write about an event with the distance fiction demands until ten years pass.

I feel I'm talking to beat sixty, a phrase he favors, from the chair in front of his desk—a bastion of oak he rests behind in a swivel chair, tilting back, hands clasped behind his neck, elbows out, assessing me. My novel will soon be in galleys (so I say), and he wonders if I will allow a movie to be made of it, if the opportunity should arise. "It's an entirely different arena," he says.

"That's how I see it—entirely separate from the book itself," I say. "I'd stay clear of what was done, I think."

"I would."

He draws a hand over a cheek—best attended to in its biting insistence on the right word—and says in his quiet, whispery voice, "When the French edition of *The Folded Leaf* was published I discovered the translator had thrown out my Middle Western dialogue and substituted French schoolboy slang instead. Nothing made a thimble of sense! So no more translations of my books. And nobody is allowed to make a movie or television spectacle out of my novels or any stories I've written. That's my stand. It's down in writing. Willa Cather had a literary executor who did her bidding and burned the manuscript of the book she was working on when she died. We should all be so well served."

Actually, Care and I have hoped for a movie contract, for the freedom it would give us to do as we wish and write what we want. "It's a lot to think about," I say, noncommittal.

"With one book out in a matter of months and another on the way, yes, I should say so." I sense perhaps a note of glory from him in saying this.

"That's what I mean."

"Just take care of your dear wife and daughter for right now and, until your first galleys appear, float."

"This time I hear you."

We both laugh. Four years ago he phoned and asked me to come up to his office so he could tell me in person the magazine had taken my first story, and then said, "Float." Meaning I should feel suspended in ether, and either I didn't hear or understand until he explained what he was saying.

"I will," I say, and rise with a hand on the back of my chair, in order to revolve and slide it under the table behind, as I've done a dozen times. This is the table where I spent long afternoons, days, weeks, at his side, working on galleys of a story or improving another on the way to proofs, and I have a fear of saying goodbye to this place of communal labor, with the shadow of his head resting over a column of words of mine set in galley type.

"Oh, you'll be back!" he says, and in a rush he's around the desk, strands of hair helter-skelter in his hurry, and as he shakes my hand he wraps the fingers of the other around my wrist. The grip to my wrist feels firmer, and his attractive teeth appear in a smile that seems to me, somehow, tentative.

And now I leap a decade ahead to another community we encountered the year we moved here and ran afoul of the laws that would affect your education as well as Newlyn's, and your younger sisters down the line. A group of parents rallied to our discontent and together we formed a private school—an academy, we called it, using a biblical name, to signify our separation from the state—and for a group of adults of such diverse beliefs to agree on a set of bylaws seemed to me a true expression of community. A sheriff arrived and threatened the students and teachers (ours with master's degrees, a higher standard than the state's) with jail, but a lawyer was on our board, his office one building down from the school, and he told the sheriff he had to follow the proper legal procedures.

Every father with a child in school was indicted and summoned to appear in court. A new state's attorney held a conference with us before our court date and said that if we disbanded and enrolled our children in the public school, he would drop the charges. "Taking this route," he said, "the next thing you'll be wanting is for them to handle poisonous snakes."

I felt it would be fair to say, "I imagine that's what they said to Catholics when they started parochial schools," since I was raised a Catholic, like the lawyer, although at that time he attended a church more socially attuned, but I saw in him a glint of the ambition and retributory malice I've seen in certain writers and critics, and kept silent. That was our lawyers' counsel: *Remain silent.*

After several days of trying to match the faces to the names on the charges (a woman from the election board, who presided at the roll I signed in the fall, pointed to somebody else when asked to identify me), the young state's attorney, now the prosecutor, had to call our wives to the stand to identify us. The trial lasted a week, and after each session the state's attorney telephoned a reporter at a regional daily newspaper and gave his view of events, and that was the next day's news.

The judge sat back in amusement at the quality of our special witnesses, who didn't merely rattle off statistics, although they could do that, but gave intelligent testimony about teaching and education—one from California quoting Greek and Hebrew traditions, and, after he used a word in one of those languages, turned to the court reporter with debonair deference and spelled it out for him. When the moment came for the judge's decision he leaned over his bench with a stern look and said, "According to the North Dakota Century Code, I can do no other than find you all guilty as charged. And I hereby fine you ten dollars apiece."

The state's attorney leaped to his feet, crying out in protest, the public school superintendent on his feet beside him, saying, "Why—!" but the judge made a swift exit out a door behind his bench. He later said the law was stupid and antiquated and needed to be changed, and a growing community began to speak to the state legislators, as we had been doing, but without the inducement of lobbyists with money.

A former headmaster of a private school in Park Forest, Illinois, a native with eminent qualifications, was back in the state, planning to run for state superintendent of public instruction, an elected office. He came to our group and said if we helped with his election he would be able, as he interpreted the Century Code, to "kind of wave a wand" and call our school certified, and he would do that. He was elected, he did that, and the school went on.

By that time we were in New York State for the school year, and after seven further years of pressure the law that essentially consecrated the Office of Public Instruction as the Commissariat of State Education was changed. The change came about at last because out-of-state groups aided in the lobbying effort, gathering one year on the capitol steps, where a few from North Dakota, as if in fear of being arrested, wore paper bags over their heads.

With my first novel out, the English Department at Urbana invited me to give a reading, and once again I entered its community of thirty thousand. I talked with Kerker Quinn, founder and editor of *Accent*, the quarterly that first published William Gass and J. F. Powers and Flannery O'Connor and Frank Holwerda, along with the instructors who oversaw the writing workshops I attended, George Scouffas and Dan Curley and Rocco Fumento and John Nims, besides a group of grad students still busy writing, and a favorite instructor in Victorian literature, Donald Smalley, plus dozens of actors and technicians I once worked with in the theater.

I went to the house of Dr. Charles Shattuck, a college friend of Maxwell—he called him Chuck—as I have to be careful not to call you, Joseph. Shattuck was an authority on the staging of Shakespeare, with several books out on noted productions, two of them winning prizes from the Folger, and the best director of Shakespeare I worked with. He lived in a scholar's humble house behind a sheep-wire fence entangled with morning glories, met me in the kitchen, where the cabinets and linoleum had the dark tone of the fifties, and sat on a stool facing me, in a blaze of sun from a window behind, so I saw him outlined in light, with shafts of sun shifting over his edges as we spoke. He brought up J. F. Powers and how he worked with Powers when he was an editor at *Accent*, and thought him such a fine fellow—this in the wake of Powers receiving the National Book Award for *Morte d'Urban*.

"He phoned and said, 'I can't say how good it feels, after the obscurity that dogged me since *Prince of Darkness* and those wonderful things we did with cats and the rest—a kind of comeuppance. *Now they'll have to sit up and take notice*, I figure.' He called after the award ceremonies and said he was as dazzled by the city as a farm boy and got lost in the building where the ceremony was held, with crowds going left and right and every which way. So he went up to an officious-looking fellow at a set of doors. This thug had a piece of paper in one hand and was ordering people hither and yon. 'Pardon me,' Powers said to him. 'I believe I'm scheduled to appear. I am J. F. Powers.'

"'Powers!' the man said, and looked up and down his list. 'Powers, Powers . . . What was the first name?' So the award made not one iota of difference to anybody, Powers said, except maybe his family—such a sweet guy!"

The sun has shifted, turning his face from a sunlit outline to the shadowy clarity of flesh, and he gives me a cheery smile. Between his fingers he grips the neck of a 7-Up and swings it like a pendulum that has placed him, since our last talk, on the other side of cigarettes and alcohol, as he's said, and with this I remember the cigarette holder he used to use with the grace and aplomb of FDR. "Doctor's orders," he says. "No more of either of my long-adored pleasures."

I'm a bit stung at hearing about Powers without a mention of my book, the reason I'm in town, but I don't detect uneasiness in him or the less salubrious side of age, envy, and after several long silences, I understand it's time to go. I get up to leave and he is on his feet: "Well, uh, Larry, *keep up with yourself!*"

The words enter me so fully they seem printed in italics, although I can't say for sure what he means by them until years down the line, when unfinished stories start to accumulate, a manuscript rack of them, besides novels I set aside when galleys or a paying project came along, with the best intentions to return to them, besides the draft of another thick novel, not to mention correspondence—or teaching or riding a tractor or fixing fence.

And it isn't until decades later, near his death, when I feel out of touch and dial his number, as one had to do then, and in the midst of our talk mention how much his piece of advice meant to me, and how I wished I had paid more attention to it at the time.

"What was it you say I said?"

I repeated the sentence for him: *Keep up with yourself.*

"How odd," he said. "Or should I say, 'Ha, ha, isn't that funny!'? Because I don't recall saying anything of the kind to you. In fact, not to anybody, ever."

So the present can obscure a truth that seemed a light and guide. In this present, the time of the PTO, a friend in our community says I should ask the nurse-practitioner who is treating me about wearing a chest binder over my ribs, to control their grating together when I stoop or lie down, so I do, and she endorses the idea. The binder is a wide elasticized band that encircles me like a bra or, more pointedly, a bandeau, the tight-fitting breast reducer of the 1920s, when the cultural style, for the body, too, was not to outshine another, or to be the lesser, and the well-endowed hid themselves in back rooms.

10

A Poet's Place

———

March 2006. Now I am alone, a peasant slave to work undone on every side, the only human being in three square miles from 8:00 AM till 6:00 at night. That's when your mother returns from work. These days light still enlivens the west as she arrives, when for a winter stretch the sky was dark by four. We embrace like lovers separated by caste or class or parents of the kind we've been, enwrapping every attribute, including our less commendable ones, in all-forgiving age.

Fourteen horses to feed keeps me busy, along with a dog and cats who need food and daily water, too, through months of freeze. I carry hay and oats to Buddy, bay stud, isolated from the mares until he's needed, which will be less often, I imagine, with a herd our size, and make my rounds in silence, groaning at a pinch of pain beside my heart, the knot of the overlapped rib, or the pull of too much weight on that arm.

On still days I pause, head raised, and listen with a concentration that causes my ears to take on the sway of radar. Usually it's only the horses' lush gnawing or an upsurge of wind. But then again, isn't solitude, a fine and private place free of interruptions from Porlock and others, with work and meditation moving ahead in harmony, what a poet wants? Some do. Others prefer the chafe of company, the stimulus of being at the center of a crowd, until the urge hits, then it's *Out of my way, I've got writing to do!*

Wherever I turn I see racks and folders and files of set-aside stories and poems and essays and books that, given the time, I hope will enter the light of the world or, as in a title Marilyn Nelson uses, *the fields of praise.* It may be pertinacious but I suspect that when the files and stacks step into print, those who complain, mostly mildly, about the years between books will feel they're coming out too fast and so can't be much good, as if I haven't been trying for years to bring them to a level the majority in me can affirm.

So I am a rogue if I do or if I don't, and the peasant slave I encounter on my tour of chores is usually glad. He and I are grateful for the partnership that wrings from us the variety of bound pages called books. And I'm sole owner and agent of the company (or touring troupe) I maintain, and a hard taskmaster makes the worse sort of slave, as one of the members of the troupe observed in a novel the entourage of us set in print in 1975.

So I'm not alone, considering my inner crew, besides the animals with their demands. On certain days the presence that enabled me to free myself from the PTO appears at my side in cell-enlivening intensity, radiating from the soles of my feet upward. When Maxwell died in 2000 at the age of ninety-two, and a few months later I had a question I wanted to ask him, I hit my desk with my fist and cried, "I can't believe he's not here!" a similar presence swept into place at my right, where he sat when we edited galleys, and he said in his whispery voice, *Oh, I'm here, Larry.*

Indeed, I've carried him so long in my head, hearing his voice giving advice, sensing him at my shoulder as I edit, we're as good as one. The loss he endured after his mother's death abraded his nature, his sensitivity, his emotional volatility (however you categorize it) and served like a Geiger counter to detect emotional falsity in writing—at least as effective as Hemingway's "built-in bullshit detector," which didn't always work, especially when Hemingway stood at a lectern in later life to draft his prose, as if proclaiming it, his writing writing at its best when he avoids the repetitious anxiety he inherited from Gertrude Stein.

"Every tear in fiction," Maxwell insisted, "has to be different from any other." I see the direction of his advice in the work of Updike, although it's present also in early Salinger. I once asked why he no longer worked with Salinger, and he said, "Jerry and I got along fine when he was writing short fiction, the sort you see in *Nine Stories.* The longer ones I wasn't so fond of and we tended not to see eye to eye, so I suggested it might be time for him to try another editor, and he moved on to working directly with Mr. Shawn.

"I'll say the same to you if I feel I should." He leaned back, hands clasped behind his head. "With *Catcher in the Rye,* he came to our place in the country when it was done and sat on the porch and read it straight through to Emmy and me. He sent it on to his publisher and assumed it would move ahead like any other book, but an editor said to him about Holden, 'That kid is crazy!' Jerry was so hurt he took the manuscript from them and published the book at another house."

Poets and writers are as various as horses, with their high-strung nature and ability to shoulder others aside for the oats. Maxwell said about Updike, "John was such a witty, intelligent young man, the kind who, like a cat, always landed on his feet. He used to stay at our apartment, early on, when he came to the city. Rumors rose about that and I'll only say that through the whole session of this we found any denial only inflames the parties bent on doing harm. There's no defense against slander, so the best defense is silence. Mediocrity cannot bear actual accomplishment."

He was the only editor I trusted to study every sentence with precision and passion, plus a liberating mercy. "No, no, leave it as it was, your instincts are right." And now as I finish this book, Joseph, he goes over every phrase from his room of residence at the rear of my head.

When we said goodbye in his office on the twentieth floor of the Graybar Building, I was bidding farewell, I felt, to the city, which he had come to embody—from his start as a young man from the Midwest immersed in its caldron, to his status as a literary elder and adjudicator, as dross was purged away by professionals on all sides. Not many editors were as well-read in every direction, and when comic metafiction began to appear in the magazine, most of which, he said, set his teeth on edge, he never implied it shouldn't have equal concourse with the writing he preferred, from the eerie fairy stories of Sylvia Townsend Warner to the rambunctious sleight of Nabokov to Updike's elegant canter. His stance was to preserve the individual integrity of the writer and, once that was set, see that each got well paid.

At Dad's, in Illinois, the absence of Maxwell sits in my mouth like the sooty atmosphere of Times Square. I keep thinking, in an echo of the start of that unfathomable play by Shakespeare, *I do not know why I am so sad.* It has to do with *What I'm Going to Do*, done and en route to print, or in part it does. My sense of the book is of a void I can't enter to alter a word, a shield between me and Care and Newlyn and my work, holding me from them and my former self.

The true sad decline, it seems now, seen from this side, is how I blame my state on where we live, which means him, *Dad.* He helps me set up an office in a back bedroom and turns his house, with a forty-foot living room, over to us. I tell him this is too much, we don't want to take over, he must keep his bedroom, and he says, "I haven't slept in it since Lorraine died." His helpless, selfless nature sets me off. I see him when he wakes (as I go off to bed) and not long after I'm up he's back from school and tries to talk to me until it's time for him to go to sleep, while I try to work, and all this stirs up adolescent irritation at the way he does or says things, which is not my way.

He lives in the basement, in a corner bedroom, his clothes stored in a dresser and a closet, and sleeps on a twin bed so ancient it sags like an old sock. He approves of our diet of organic food and supplements and takes to your mother's cooking with a husbandly savor, which causes an oedipal quake. He gets back from school as soon as he can, in suit and tie, and rubs his hands in eagerness for the evening meal, and then he grips his left hand in a fist on the table as he eats. My retaliation is to drink too much, which he hates.

Newlyn is usually in the kitchen, lying on a mat on the floor with her toys close, showing how she can push up to hold her head erect, *bob, bob, bob,* or sit in her high chair, her eyes on Care at work as she snacks, food down her chin and bib. Dad pokes her side with a finger and speaks nonsense like "A *goo* boo-boo," although I told him we want to avoid baby talk and speak to her as we would a normal person.

She screeches at his pokes and fooling and, if she's on her mat, rolls on her back, her arms out, and kicks both legs in a way that causes her jumper to appear elastic, springing her ahead as she whoops. In her high chair she bends over with such force at her laughter she bangs her head on its tray. Then she bangs it on purpose, squealing with delight.

I've developed a hypersensitivity to sound, minus hers, most of the time, especially unexpected noise and, much worse, unnecessary repetitive noise—snapping gum, clicking a ball point, humming, drumming fingers: his nails always long. And why does he speak to Newlyn as he does, when in every instance from the past that I can remember I hear his pure enunciation in the sonorous golden melancholy of A. E. Housman?

If I happen to be in the house or hear him from the room where I work (on a door I used as my desk in New York), I go to the high chair and pluck Newlyn from it and walk with her through the house or sit in a rocker in the living room and read one of her books to her, several sent by Michael, who also edits children's books. My favorites are *Goodnight Moon* and *The Little Fur Family*, with its fuzzy cover of fur Newlyn likes to stroke, then bite.

Quitting smoking is a goal. For weeks I was fine but now I puff and gnaw at the wooden tip of a Swisher Sweet, chewing its sugar-soaked tip to splinters, drooling as I type. Most mornings Dad and I encounter each other as he prepares for school, a percolator on the counter thumping with the sound of Newlyn's fist on her high-chair tray, and I walk in from a night of work that has ended in bright day, dazed. He looks bleary-eyed and dazed, too, a surprise, since he was always the first up, early enough to drive fifty miles to work if he was on a plastering crew, or arrive at school an hour before the opening study hall to prepare announcements for the day, his actor's voice resounding in every corner of the spacious assembly hall.

I get glimpses of the look that overcame him when he did the dishes, alone, now with a new far-off strain to it, although I wasn't up with him when I was in high school and had to force my way out of bed after a night up late to write (my writing began then), with hardly a half hour to spare, just time to dress and brush my teeth and head for school with a glance down the block for my tardy mistress, as I thought of her, to see how close she was, since her habit was to hold back in her walk until I showed up—Camilla Magee, I'll call her—her family outcasts according to small-town standards, where the idea was anybody with gumption could get a job at Caterpillar or Quaker Oats or Keystone Steel and Wire in Peoria, forty miles off. Of course, you had to have a car to do that.

She was bright, witty, the sort of student my father favored in a system that equated financial hardship with lack of intellect. She was looked down on or ignored, her frizzy hair fixed with too many bobby pins, off-color teeth that seemed dead from family circumstance, dresses out of fashion, perhaps a sister's, smiling at me with the fond and bitter tinge of household affection. The two of us would slip through the heavy doors and in a hurried patter go up the steps to the all-school assembly, under the skylights of the third floor, and stand at a radiator, staring through an arch at Dad's back and the faces of students at their desks, and when he is done and turns to us in the uproar of movement for the day's first class, we have to ask him to cross off our names as absent, since we're present, though late, and he says to me once at home, "I would think you'd try to get to school a little earlier, maybe for my sake," with a mildness I attribute to Camilla. No, I never even kissed her, carrying at least a partial understanding of taking advantage.

Work doesn't go well in his house. I try to draft the story of a man who comes home after the death of his father and takes on, literally, his burial—a story whose end I saw on a New York subway—but only fragments appear, as if I'm pulling scraps from a fire growing by leaps. I get down the sound, *ba bee, ba bee* of a windowpane in the room where I work and then feel stalled. I start drafting a new scene that enters the rear of my mind in movie-like fashion, stuttering and slowed, as if an antiquated projector is running down—a flashing conjunction of legs in a race and a boy being lifted above a crowd—and I know this will be the end of the story, in the way endings always appear to me first. But I can't get it going to reach the scene I've glimpsed, and I grab the pages I've been working on and throw them across the room.

I start a piece about a pair of boys hired by a widow to kill the cats overrunning her barn, and it pours from a point of view that takes such swift turns I call it "shifting surface texture." But as the boys enter the barn where they plan to begin their kills, my mind curves like the hasp of a padlock and clicks in place, frozen at the thought. I start typing what I've drafted, hoping to roll past that point, but when I get near the end of the last handwritten page sweat springs over my forehead and I toss the typewriter high in the air as if I've been shocked.

And notice Newlyn on her mat behind, playing in such a quiet way I've forgotten her, Care out shopping, and catch the Selectric I got in order to type up *What I'm Going to Do* (and still make payments on), before it hits down. She erupts in giggles as if Dad has poked her. A memory hits home: the fall Care and I moved to our apartment, I started a new novel, setting aside for the moment the one Maxwell referred to as *My Brother's Visit to New York*—my first go at a novel—which I had set aside earlier to write a story that was the first the *New Yorker* took, and then others began to accumulate and take on the contours of the scenes I saw the night in Urbana in my contemplation of *Hamlet,* every one a chapter of the book I must now finish, *Beyond the Bedroom Wall*—all this backtracking and layering loops maddening!—and I flung an antique upright Underwood in New York in the midst of that.

From a waist-high file where I keep starts and scenes of unfinished work in slide-out trays, I pull out the chapters of that "first" novel and page to a section I feel sure will work as a story. Leaps in income along with sudden lacks have added new pressure, once I moved from stories to books, but here this is. I type up the section and send it to Maxwell and in a week hear back—won't work, he says, without sending it on to other editors at the magazine.

I pull out a notebook I kept over my first year in New York, for the help I hoped it would be, as if I expect to find dirt on him, and come across a dream:

In jail. In prison.

The escape. 3 men—a woman

1 woman knifed by guard—she wasn't guilty or in on the escape, just with them

I wasn't one of them, but wanted to watch—see if they escaped. In order to keep up I identified with one. He was leading the break. He had a gun.

All are shot by the guard but him.

Then I know he isn't the hero and will be shot.

The justification for his death comes out of the guard's mouth and travels down his arm and comes out with the bullet—the young man has killed his father—and now the guard is saying as in a badly written book, or comic book, "This is for all the good fathers like your father was . . ."

And on and on.

And then he fired. The bullet hit the man I had identified with . . . , or me, in the head. It woke me up. I can still feel the weight of it . . . When I was hit, I just had time to say from the Lord's Prayer "Our Father" before I died.

I drop the notebook and go to the kitchen, where Care is starting dinner, and see Newlyn has her head on her high-chair tray, turned to the side to sleep, and stop with such force Care turns as if I've spun her around to face me.

"We've got to get out of here," I say. "Let's go."

. . .

It's a place that Carole's family used to rent, on Lake Michigan. She is busy with photography and for my birthday gives me an enlargement: in a suit jacket and watch cap I stand between two birches—a younger one, behind, spreads a network of limbs over the lake and sky, and I stand at an odd angle in order to brace myself against the wind, which keeps up such a velocity over the season it feels like streamers of gauze over my ears, creating a whorling headful of noise.

From my notebook:

> While I was helping a farmer-poet down the road get in
> his field corn, Carole was preparing a surprise birthday
> party. She cleaned and decorated the cabin, made a cake, a
> meal, stocked us with a case of Heinekens and a fifth of Old
> Granddad, got gifts and supplies, and had five guests here
> and candles going when I got back, and she did it all with
> Newlyn in arms and twenty bucks. Jim and Linda Harrison
> were here, with friends. I'd wanted to meet Harrison for a
> while and it was good of him to be here, because he just got in
> that morning from New York, where he was promoting his
> new quarterly, Sumac. When I walked in the door he was
> standing in the living room, the only one visible, broad, cor-
> pulent, with a dark walrus mustache and wide round face, a
> drink in hand, and I immediately knew it was him. I greeted
> everybody and asked to first clean up, stinky with sweat, and
> he said, "Don't use underarm deodorant, L! It'll give you
> cancer!" He is calm and mordant, as in sense of humor, and
> when he speaks, showing a wide set of widely spaced teeth
> under the dark mustache, he speaks in a breathy wheeze, as if
> he were using his last lungful of air, and speaks slooow-lee. It

makes each word suspenseful and precise. He's a Buddha,
hair buzzed off. The quality of him was summed up in a
sentence; I had been holding Newlyn on my lap, talking,
or holding forth, rather, and had finally begun to eat (she
loves to sit with me while I eat) Carole's luscious Garbure,
my favorite meal, when he said, as naturally as hello, "Do
you want me to hold Newlyn for you?"

I'm saved from worry about where to turn when the galleys
of my novel arrive, narrow and floppy, two feet long, with the
indentation of the linotype letters creating an impression of
Braille across every line on the sheets. I sit at a table and begin
the pleasant task.

On the phone a gruff and wheezy voice says so slowly it
seems to set a triple space between words, "Can we come up
on your hill and hunt, uh, birdies? Harrison. My buddy Tom
is here for the week and we'd love to come up to your hill and
hunt. Quail, sharp-tail, woodcock, *ummm.* You got woodcock?
Love that breast!"

Care, attuned to wildlife, wonders if it's OK to invite hunters to a place where we're guests, and I tell her in a wind like
this they won't hit a cow. A while later, from the window where
I work, I see Harrison and an electrically skinny fellow, both
dressed in canvas hunting garb, draw shotguns from a station
wagon I didn't hear drive up. The wind.

Tom is Tom McGuane, heir to Hemingway, according to
those who know him, with an inhumanly perfect eye able to
identify a bird at a quarter of a mile, a hawk at a half, so the stories
go, with his first novel on its way to publication after a year in
Spain. We shake and say hello as a swirl of dogs in clattering

tags, one with liver-colored markings, circles us, and McGuane, a strawberry redhead with high color, lifts a tubular whistle from his neck and blows. They stop and sit. His canvas trousers are leathered over the front and look rigged by Abercrombie and Fitch. Harrison moves back as we talk and his bad eye, or artificial one, the original lost when a schoolmate stabbed it with a pencil, waters as he smiles.

I walk with them and their dogs to the edge of an orchard and tell them the land is somebody else's, and perhaps they shouldn't hunt here. In his slow setting of each word in place, Harrison says, "We asked. His answer was, 'Go ahead.'"

"Northern Spies!" McGuane says, and steps to a tree where apples weigh lower branches to the ground. He ponders a group high up, held in a cluster like the solution to a question in math, rocking with the wind. He cradles his shotgun in his arm, barrel above his head, an athlete attuned to distances, and with the hand of the arm cradling the gun holds a cluster of apples steady, plucks one loose, and takes a deep bite. "There's nothing like a ripe apple fresh off the tree in fall air and, *yum*, a Northern Spy!"

He smiles as he speaks, nodding in self-agreement as he chews, and something about his rose-auburn complexion and the length of his face and high-powered eyes conveys the impression of a thoroughbred nodding and gnawing at a bit it intends to bite on and run. They go off and I keep my distance, wary of the sawing action of shotguns walked, and in the crowns of trees above I see windblown leaves reverse like sprung umbrellas, ribs visible, and at the base of the wind I hear *thup thup* as they fire at something I can't see. Their dogs hop on hind legs like rabbits to see above the grass, ears flapping, then tear off until the whistle holds them up.

McGuane turns and slowly shakes his head.

At the edge of a field a line of second growth runs along a ridge above the lake. The two stand at its edge and when I walk up McGuane says, "I was saying somebody should perfect a breed of dog so you could say, 'Scout through this, Scout, and scare up some birds,' and he would."

"I will." The brush is twice my height and I paw my way into it until I can barely see the two, then work my way back through, a forearm up, and when I have to struggle at the edge to get out, finally dropping to my hands and knees, a dog indeed now, to slip below entangling branches, it seems the barrels of their guns are trained on me. *(Not then, but now I think of the malign hatred I've seen in writers and critics, not the two with shotguns, but the sort about whom John Gardner wrote, "Some kill with a gun and others with words," who will attack not a book but the person who wrote it with deadly intent, no scruples, falsifying even the content or the outlook of a character to make you appear stupid, a fool, one as well done away with, and don't think it isn't so, and I wonder . . .)*

No, they hold them in the crooks of their arms, barrels turned aside, though both are studying me.

"I hear you have stories in the *New Yorker*," McGuane says.

Why do I feel cornered when a writer asks this, after the decompression I go through (more often lately) about the most recent maybe being my last? "I have," I say, though I know several are idling at the moment in the magazine's bank.

Tears run from Harrison's slow-moving eye and with a stroke of a knuckle under it, he says, "How does it feel to have troughs of your prose winding through all those ads?"

"If that's the way they pay you what they do, fine."

McGuane asks how much that is.

When I say it varies, he says, "Hit me with an average."

I do and he says, "Jeez, why didn't you send me some!" He laughs, his Adam's apple jogging in his throat, and a flush swells through his face. "What's your novel about?"

"I have galleys if you want to see a chapter."

"My galleys came a while back. Isn't it great to be a real writer?" I see only enthusiasm in him and think of the stories I've published, the poems, the novel in galleys, the others half done or on the way, and I'm not sure I feel like a real writer— rather like one who keeps on. I want to explain this but hold out my hand. We end with a gentlemanly shake.

I sit alone on the lawn, my back against a tree, in a wind that imitates Lear's howl, sending leaves sailing past in such quick streaks it's hard to discern their color, while those that remain chatter with an insistence that penetrates the surface deafness smothering me. Birds blow past, wings flitting or racked by the wind, tilting crazily, about to hit the end of things, the way it looks, and I know I can't go on like this, with bills unpaid, so that I feel I'm a petty evasive crook, and can't continue to pretend whatever I do will in any way be assuaged or abetted by alcohol, only destroyed, so I can't continue to drink, for the sake of Care and Newlyn and Dad, the wind trebling so the canals of my ears quake with the effort to hear as I see my desk in the room Dad helped set up, my sense of hearing so over-whelmed I'm able only to see and I see my hand moving forward on the story of a father burying *his* father, lines and loops forming words under the pencil lead. Then an overlay of the flashing legs arrives, the race I visualized with a boy at its end hoisted above a crowd with a roar like the wind, and a sentence that's been revolving in me is, I know, the start of that story, which is the start of my novel, the book I need to finish, and in the deafness created by the wind I see the sentence say: *Every night when I'm unable to sleep, when pages of words and formulas uncoil in my mind and the faces of people I love, living and dead, rise from the dark, accusing me of ambition, self-regard, hostility, neglect—whatever their accusations are, all of them just—and I know there's no hope of rest, I try to picture the street where a boy once ran a race.*

I run inside to write this down, into the stereophonic amplitude of silence of enclosure in that room, and I'm back to March 2005 and the room where I sit alone, thinking of our horses and hearing their multiplied gnawing. Ranchers walk through chores at the same time each day, in the same pattern, so the thought doesn't occur, *Oh, I have to do this again*—merely pull on a coat and go at it, their stock never running along a fence, bellowing or neighing, or pawing at a trough or water tank, no yowling cat or dog outside to remind you they, too, must be fed. The bounty of chores, Joseph, is their power to remind you of the necessity of seeing to others.

No time is wasted bowing to Number One.

One horse crowds the others, nips and kicks at them, and takes such big gulps of oats her cheeks fill and grainy saliva slobbers from her lips into the trough. I take a training whip, a popper, not the type that hurts, to try to instill restraint in her, but no go. I walk into the pen to chase her off and she crowds half a dozen horses sideways instead of backing out from them. I throw frozen horse apples and an empty plastic pail at her, and the next day it's as if nothing has happened: one of those that never learn.

We dislike seeing in others, including animal analogues, who we are. No act connects with us as a fault unless we have it by heart. We can only judge what we recognize and we recognize only what we know and that's what we're made of.

For a term in the 1980s, western North Dakota was suffering a drought, with only an inch of rain over thirteen months, and we couldn't raise enough grain to show a profit, only enough to feed a university for a year. I was in the midst of another book that seemed to have *Endless* written across it and had to set it aside for essays and reviews to keep the utilities paid, and if I ever happen to say, "There was one winter—" Laurel jumps in with, "Yes, we know," meaning she's heard the story too many times. That winter we ate our own wheat, cracked as cereal for breakfast, baked into bread that was the staple of the rest of our meals, with a jar of canned fruit or berries brought up from the basement once a week. If it hadn't been for a friend who hoped I would write a book for him, our farm would have gone to the bank.

The Welsh poet Dylan Thomas used to say that the only proper position for a poet to maintain is upright, which might not be so amusing if you didn't know how often he was falling-down drunk. He may have heard the phrase when he ran with the Dadaists and learned about Edvard Munch, the Norwegian painter known for *The Scream,* who said, "The second half of my life has been a battle just to keep myself upright." An artist's struggle for equipoise is always in a given place or, to paraphrase an Updike poem, *Watch it, writer, when your place narrows to the room where you sit.*

A gift from a relative was displayed on our kitchen wall that winter, a print of a white-bearded man in a work shirt at a table with his hands clasped and head bowed over a crust of bread, a Scandinavian Stoic, as I thought of him, and then thought, *My God, it's come true!*—careful of how I ate, for our children's sake.

But the winter must have left its imprint, because as our children grew and gained adult appetites, I dug in quick to make sure of a second helping, reverting to my first family's daily battle for food as Dad tried to keep order at the table. These days I would fast if I could sit at a meal with my family again.

And if I were to include the person I excluded most of my life, because I saw myself so clearly in him that I became his judge and arbiter and began to believe, as my work moved on, that I was his superior, it would be my father. The sting of the shame of that, Joseph, is partly purged by setting in place for you the truth of who I am.

II

Not Giving In

―――――

You would not give in, Joseph, a quality that grew in you as you matured. You would not get down on your hands and knees to crawl across a floor when the act of sitting and drawing yourself ahead with your feet was more regal, and you would not give in to your older sister when you realized she did not have the authority of your mother, and you would not give up baking bread or disassembling kitchen machines.

You worked at repairs with your face so close you seemed drawn inside the internal mechanism, your body rocking with a wrench to a rhythm ingrained in the stars, or rather the revolution of the earth that swings them into shining array. Your focus didn't waver until the fix was perfect and true, in line, fastened so tight I couldn't loosen a bolt once you passed fifteen. You didn't give in when your first bicycle kept crashing but remounted and mastered the skill in a day.

You would not give in after the horse took you into the long drench of lost consciousness, and when the specialist at NYU said that whatever we were doing we should keep it up, we could have said it was because you would not give in.

When the doc who worked on your fingers noticed during an office visit that the pins in two were loose and took hold of your hand and with his own fingers extracted them—like narrow knitting needles—from where they protruded, you didn't cry out, but his act triggered a bone infection that required intravenous antibiotics; you would not give up soccer when friends gathered for a game, though you carried a shunt in your arm that had to be plugged into an IV every afternoon, and would not listen when I tried to restrain you from the weekly softball game a group of us played that summer in our front hayfield.

It was the area you were mowing when you reached to re-hook the platform. And if you endured a weight of guilt about that, mine overarched it like cloud cover, when it should have been the shadow of wings you were resting under, as in Psalms, a shield from harm, an otherworldly protection that the best of fathers provide.

My interweaving is on purpose, with the hope of holding you in one of its stopped-moments for a momentary glimpse of your own infinity. All experience is simultaneous, stilled and sealed in itself, and we manage daily by imagining we move from minute to minute, somehow always ahead. Our multiple selves collide at every second of intersection, one or the other vying for supremacy, the scars of the past flooding through the present texture of our personality, and maturity is knowing how to govern the best combination of them.

· · ·

I picture you on a recent visit, walking the fields you worked for a decade with your son Timothy at your side, and the angle your arm takes to hold his raised hand trips my memory into an avalanche, and I'm displaced to the year we arrived, when the family would lie below the lilacs at the edge of the yard on blankets your mother spread on the grass, inhaling a scent of chlorophyll and wool, and you would roll on your back and reach for the cumulus piled in an illusion of mountainous cascades overhead as if you could pluck down a cloud in your plump hand, while for me it was another day of guiding the Allis with its belly mower in a crawl across the farm, a small haystack to skirt in the front field, a leftover from the Berns of another time and place—a thumbprint of hay mounded in a European manner—the hayfield of crested wheat, seed from the Russian steppes, lying between a Siberian pea-tree hedge and a row of ash, its far edge slanting to a falloff of terraced clay forty feet to the road. The grass bent so far back under the force of the fall wind the sickle bar rode over its top, going with the grain, barely clipping on those passes, but every second I spent in the aroma of gasoline exhaust baking on the manifold and muffler (glowing orange as the afterglow dimmed to night) was a wink of eternity, presaging our new life.

And now you walk with your son's hand in yours and I see in the angle of your body the weight on you of a recent report that Timothy is autistic—a mild autism he will likely grow out of, you've been told, but you're hurt, impatient that he's not like other children, angry at him and yourself, and I want to tell you I was like him, I was like him, Joseph, and being patient with him is a way of coming to bear with the failings in me.

. . .

The work in Michigan does not go well, so we move back to
Dad's, the cold feet of irresolution plunged in adamant prison.
Candida calls to say one of her brainy, bratty boys, one I met in
her office, wants the movie option on *What I'm Going to Do, I
Think.* Give it, I say. Roger Straus calls to tell me he's planning
a publication party; the novel is a Literary Guild selection and
is going into its fourth printing. "Let's make it May 9," I say,
Newlyn's birthday, and so it's set.

I want to go, but now I don't want to leave Dad's. I've finished a new chapter, "The Old Halvorson Place," I've finished
the story of the boys and the cats, and I have the opening pages
of a Neumiller daughter at Christmas. I want to get back to
"The Burial," which I feel ready for, and now Care says I need a
new suit and Dad says I should see a local tailor, Zygmunt. I do
and choose a fabric of electric green, with blue pinstripes. We
send Roger names of people to invite and soon we're checked
into the St. Regis, a hotel I admired on my city walks.

The newest Cheever book, *Bullet Park,* is waiting at the desk,
sent by messenger from Candida—he's one of her clients. It has
received tepid reviews, besides a bomb in the *New York Times,*
and I sit and read it straight through and in the morning send
Cheever a cheering telegram.

I call my buddy Bob De Niro, who can't make the party,
he says, because of a tryout, and wants me to know he's with
a new woman, this one permanent. We can bring Newlyn to
his place, he says, and they'll babysit for us. We dress for the
night, my first excursion in the tailored skin of emerald green
and tailored shirt with a sixties silk collar, and head for Bob's.
The permanent new woman is tall and striking, with the high
forehead and features of Ethiopian aristocracy and a settled
serenity in her smile.

"Wow!" Bob says. "That suit!"

Carole settles Newlyn, half asleep, on the floor near the front windows, on her blanket, and says it's probably the best place, safe, just as Newlyn turns her head to sleepily survey the other-worldly princess her mother, in her floor-length gown and jewelry and curls, has become. We go slinking out, with Bob beaming first at Newlyn, then at us, then at *her*.

"Bay-*bee!*" Roger says. "This is one night nobody's going to have trouble identifying the guest of honor! I'll say, 'Look for the guy the color of a new dollar bill!'"

I tell him it's meant to show I'm a green writer.

"Get off my back!"

His wife Dorothea, in a broad-brimmed black hat draped with a cyclorama of black lace tucked into a high collar, takes Carole to the powder room, and Roger whispers, "I'm not covering your St. Regis bill, buddy, I want you to know that. Our writers aren't on expense accounts!"

I tell him there was a foul-up with our reservation, so I had the desk clerk contact him as a reference. A living room nearly the length of the brownstone, with a step-up to a sitting area that looks out on the street, is filling with people and the din of talk. Roger introduces me to Henry Moe, who says something I can't understand because Roger is whispering the names of guests who have to leave early, and in the turns and directions he marches me, with his hands on my shoulders, I feel I'm barely hanging on.

When he releases me I make for the far end of the room, where a bar is set up and waiters in white coats are serving, and run into Wilfrid Sheed, with a leonine mane of graying hair, leaning on a cane, talking to Roger III—an affable and gentle man, built like a fullback, running ads for my book.

NOT GIVING IN205

I go over to a group of three and it turns out two are from the *New York Times*, one of whom Roger said I should meet, John Leonard, who has the foxy look of Harvard success, his thin nose pinched by wiry granny glasses—and we get in a heated discussion about *Bullet Park*, though I'm not sure how it started, and he tends to agree, he says—the *Times* reviewer was not only unsympathetic but missed the point of the book.

"It's a *fable*, for God's sake, Hammer and Nailles!"

"I'll remember this conversation when the next Cheever comes in," he says. The third fellow, not from the *Times*, a reviewer at *Newsweek*, has an elegant Southern accent tinged by Elizabethan, and over his shoulder I see handsome Susan Sontag sitting on the edge of a couch, leaning in impassioned talk to a short fellow with such a terrible scowl on his face he looks like a miniature monster. Edmund Wilson?

A stately guest with a face like Wilson's steps up and I recognize, through his wife beside him, the psychiatrist I saw in the city, later a friend, Bill Triebel. I forgot I invited him. *He's lost a hundred pounds*, I think, and feel he's gained airspace, too, high above me. He says, "I've counted fifty celebrities I recognize," and then does a fake furtive glance around and whispers, "I'm impressed by your friends." His working mode is to set the worst situation in comic relief. I tell him all New York likes Roger's parties.

"You were always modest," he says, and smiles with such benign benevolence I feel I'm in a session with him again.

My editor Michael draws me aside to meet Natalie Babel, daughter of a favorite writer discovered in college, fresh in mind after *You Must Know Everything*, which I read in galleys and preferred over his poetic depictions of Cossacks. Michael sits next to Natalie on a loveseat and as we begin to talk somebody from a chair says, "Hello, I'm Francine du Plessix Gray"—a willowy beauty I imagined as schoolmarmish, from the precision of her prose, and I tell her so. "Why do you think that is?" she asks, as if beginning an interview.

But I notice Candida, who dislikes parties as much as Maxwell (who won't be here, he's told me), curled up in an easy chair in a corner, shoes off, behind a phalanx of tall talkers, and see that the young man who has my movie rights is sitting on an arm of her chair. He gives me a thumbs-up.

Isaac Singer is pulling on a topcoat to leave and as I ponder how to say hello in goodbye, Tom Wolfe, in a white suit as sizzling as his recent book, *The Electric Kool-Aid Acid Test*, eases to my side and says with a roll of his head, "Nice suit. Who did the shirt, that collar?"

"The silk, you mean?"

"And the design—the height of the collar and its tabs of, well, a certain distinction. A shop in the city?"

"Zygmunt. Woodstock, Illinois."

"Ah!" Whatever he starts to add is lost as somebody pulls at him from the other side, and I hear Roger say from behind, "Nobody's having trouble identifying *this* guest of honor!" But a stilled bystander from the inner room fitted with an intercom whispers, *Oh? Well, I am.*

In dim light at Bob's Newlyn sleeps with her face to the wall, her legs drawn under her, rump raised, and the four of us hold a whispered conversation above her. Bob's permanent steps back, as if to give the two of us a moment together, and sits in a chair, hands clasped over a knee. Carole thanks her for her help tonight. Bob walks me to the street, the women continuing to talk as we hunt for a taxi at whatever hour it is. He takes my arm and says, "I'm going to marry her."

"That's wonderful."

He smiles and looks me over, up and down, as if hoping to hear more, planting his feet and taking the rocking swagger from the ankles of a stud. I feel stunned by the night but want to be congratulatory, and when he doesn't speak, I say, "I hear you clear. She's the one you want to marry."

"I do."

We laugh at how this comes out.

"It'll be good for you. I'm sure she'll be a help in"—I don't want to say *settling down* or *acquiring artistic depth* or *furthering your career*—"in your search."

"For what?"

"Whatever your heart desires," I say, the title of an E. B. White story that suddenly comes to me.

"That's what I got."

No, Joseph, the path to the person I'll be never ends, as it will not for you. You had the Wright brothers' urge to fly and one winter when we were in the East you leaped off the roof of the porch of our rented house into a snowbank below, unaware the snow was frozen, and jolted a leg badly. Your mother was so upset she called me at the university and asked me to deal with you when I got back. You were in your upstairs room, with its window onto the porch roof, sitting on your bed in darkness. I put my arm around you and repeated what your mother said about your jump. "Is that true?"

"Yes," you said, and I embraced you at the melancholy sound of your admission. That was it.

Then the accident at the end of the earlier memoir, when your mother and I were in Bismarck and you started to unload the pistol you kept under your mattress whenever you were alone with Ruth and Laurel, and were distracted by an announcement on the radio downstairs and went to the landing between your rooms, the pistol resting on towels and clothes for a shower, and in one of those gaffes of young men somehow tipped the towels, saw the revolver go in the tumbling slow motion of a mind working at top speed, a cheap .38 special with a faulty hammer you bought on a whim from a beekeeper you worked with, and were so sure it would fire you vaulted into a run but the slug entered the back of your leg, missing every major artery and nerve by millimeters, chipping off a piece of your kneecap, and lodged in the ceiling above your head.

Your head. That spring you were on crutches, listless, gripping the rattling aluminum prods with both handles in one hand when you sat, your head hanging, and once off them you left for Bismarck, where you worked as an apprentice mechanic to a private pilot and walked or rode a bicycle to build up your leg, and swam in the Heart River's turbulent entry into the Missouri, jumping off a railroad bridge to do that, or so somebody told me. You never did. The wounded are the last to be received with open arms, and the first to accept sacrifice.

You applied to the Air Force Academy and took their physical, which you passed until a computer put pins in your leg, contrary to X-rays and doctors' exams, and on the advice of an administrator at the academy you enrolled in a Bismarck college until the snafu was fixed. Your mother and I were surprised to hear you tried out for soccer and made the team, and attended a game in the frigid stadium, both tugging at the only blanket we brought, and saw you enter the game until a player kicked your scarred knee so hard you went down. The beast in me rose rampant in the debilitating blind anxiety known as rink rage, and I went on tremulous legs to a chain-link fence close to the bench where you were massaging your knee, and yelled, "What the hell's going on?" You turned and said in a mild way, aware of my state from the tone conveyed, "I don't think he meant it."

In February 2000, when you came to talk about tending the furnace while we were away, you told us you had decided to enlist in the Army. "*What?*" came out of both of us, "The *Army?*" They had a variety of helicopters the Air Force did not have, you said, and it was helicopters you wanted to fly.

"I thought you wanted to attend the Air Force Academy," your mother said, pained.

"No," you said. "No, *you* wanted me to attend it."

And at that moment I knew you were grown up.

So you enlisted, and when you returned, finished with Basic and advanced training, I asked you out to my office. You said the rigors of those months weren't so bad except for the hazing, inspired by a drill instructor, which became a barrier of prejudice against you that you had to work your way through. What was the worst of it? I asked.

"Mower man."

"*Mower man?*"

You mentioned a film and said, "Calling me mower man."

"Why?"

You held up your left hand, its two fingers ribbed with spiraling scars, and I wanted to take it in mine and ask you to forgive me. But I said, "You shouldn't have told them how it happened, with that lousy, ugly, broken mower. You should have said, 'That's as much chewing as the sons-a-bitch got done before I tore his tongue out.'"

"Dad! I couldn't say that. It's not true!"

I meant to launch into what I intended to say when I asked you out, but at that drew back. In my office I suspect I assume the pose of a writer, and realize this must be the mode you and your sisters saw: do not disturb. But you had a canny way of standing in attendance while you asked a question and then waited, stilled as wildlife, for a reply, draped across my easy chair in the bowed, half-lying fashion of a young man, elbows hooked on its arms, black jacket bunched in grooves of finger-worn leather, unmoving for I don't know how long until, stirred by your silence, I would say, "Sorry. I seem to keep on working while you sit right here."

"No, go on, go ahead," you would say. "I just wanted to rest here a while."

One night your fingers went to your jaw in a thoughtful pose, as for a painting in the manner of Rembrandt, one that employs his subtle tones to depict dimension, giving his final self-portraits the feel of floating molecular fields. Then I heard, *It feels good.* You didn't say it, anyway not out loud, and maybe it was my vocalized thought, but the phrase entered in your voice, *It feels good.* And I realized you were at my feet or in my arms during my creative phases and planning and designing crazes, now a young man in the drape of eighteen. The wind was working exploratory shoulders over the doors and windows on three sides and we sighed at the same time, as we do when our inner barometers reach a matching degree, and in a pattering of sensation like particles lifting from my face I felt us coincide with the shouldering edge of wind, a sharp reminder: *We built this place.*

Finally I say what I intended. "Joseph, I can't imagine having a better son. I mean, of the many sons I can imagine, I can't imagine one as good as you've been."

It doesn't come out quite as I had hoped, and you say with surprise, "Oh, thank you." We both stare at the oak floor it took a week to set in place, drilling and nailing every three-quarter-inch board above its tongue at the proper angle for nailing, and then days to finish it to its present sheen. We built this place and in it I build books and now build this one for you.

The day after Roger's party we take a suite in the St. George, in our former Brooklyn Heights neighborhood, and Bob Giroux arrives for a planned lunch—"this one on me," I say. Our meal in the hotel dining room goes well until Newlyn starts squealing and flinging food, as if to inform us what she thinks about being left alone (for the first time) with people she doesn't know, and her shrieks seem to run through Bob like javelins. He asks about my progress on the book and I feel so on edge I figure if he asks once more, "Are we going to see the children mature?" I'll say, *No, I'm making them all immature, under-developed idiots like me.* Carole, attuned to tension, plucks up Newlyn and walks off with her.

"Well," Bob says, "I was wondering if you think it might be artistically strategic to include the father's reactions to the mother's death. What we have now is only the boy's."

I hadn't thought of this, and the swarm of clamor in me subsides. "Yes, of course," I say. "You're right."

I feel a second book to the one I'm working on open from me at the table, with every generation included, the ties between them all complex and intact, as I envisioned it that night contemplating *Hamlet*, and pause to get my breath and refocus my hundred-yard stare.

We rent Ben Hecht's former house in Upper Nyack. Its central section is colonial, dating from the 1700s, but Hecht added a dining area to one side and, up a flight of stairs, a gazebo-like greenhouse and, on the other side, another house—so large its basement (excluding a furnace-maintenance room) is either a full-size gymnasium, the walls and floor lined with exercise mats, or a padded madhouse. The house itself surmounts four terraces that, on their lowest shelf, give out on a bluff overlooking the Hudson. The second terrace, down from a flagstone deck for dining, holds an Olympic-size pool, with a naked nymph at one end spouting water from her mouth at the diving board. On both sides of the next terrace, stone gazebos stand, each with a second-story studio.

The upper floor of the colonial has been converted into a modern den or television room by the family renting to us, and off it a large addition above the gymnasium rambles—a maid's room with a bedroom across the hall from it (Newlyn's room, we decide), and the rest of the upper floor is a master bedroom with a walk-in closet and dressing room larger than our previous bedrooms. A tub is built into an alcove in a far bedroom wall, with a fresco of nymphs and satyrs entwined in a sexy scene painted by Maxfield Parrish, a Hecht admirer and friend.

I'm used to working in an enclosed, cramped space, and the rooms are so large I feel my consciousness float off to fill the void. At the end of a galley kitchen is a breakfast booth I find comfortable. I turn to the story of the Neumiller sister, Marie, at Christmas, and by the time I get a paragraph down the phone rings; the fellow with the movie option wants to meet. In the midst of dinner he asks me outside, and I can't imagine what's up until he pulls out a bomber and lights up, coughing, and passes it on, and I think, *Is this the way to do business?*

If I set my pencil to a page the phone or a doorbell goes off, a young woman coming or going who helps Care in the kitchen or wades into the pool with Newlyn—able to hold herself afloat in a splashing way before she can speak. Dr. Triebel and his wife Lou and three children drive out most weekends to use the pool. They won a swimming championship at their Y—it was swimming, Triebel says, along with diet, that melted his weight. We talk about Maxwell and I say I sometimes worry about his seeing Reik for depression.

"Still that over-concern about others, eh?" Triebel asks.

He and Lou are at the table on the flagstone deck when the Maxwells arrive, Emmy a stunning beauty, Bill dapper in a summer jacket and Scots golf cap he wears when he isn't at the office—"to protect my balding head from the sun," he says, since "balding" is a word Mr. Shawn dislikes, meaning it doesn't appear in the magazine under his reign, along with "spat" (liquid through lips) and "home" and most other four-letter words—"home" too mushily sentimental.

Maxwell sits across from Triebel in the dining patio, sets his cap on the table, and says he's sure they visited this place before, in the Hecht era, as he remembered on the drive from their country house in Yorktown Heights—a night party, he thought. A story of his about a family trip to France, "The Gardens of Mont St. Michel," was reprinted that year in one of the best-of-the-year collections, and I showed it to Triebel. He begins to ask questions about the story, as if analyzing Maxwell through it, as he once did me. But Maxwell's clear, brief answers, with no backpedaling in his eyes, his face immobile, makes it clear this won't go far.

They talk about their children—Maxwell's daughters the age of Triebel's younger son and daughter—and I remind Triebel, for Maxwell's benefit, what he had said after Newlyn was born, when we asked, "If we have another child, what age is the worst for the existing one?" and he said, "Any age."

Maxwell laughs a jittery pleased laugh. "It reminds me of my older brother," he says, and tells the story of how his brother lost a leg in an accident but acted all his life as if his wooden leg were nonexistent, with a special talent to tease Maxwell, simply by a look, that caused him to cry. He laughs heartily about this childhood weakness.

After a meal of salad Niçoise Care has arranged with an artistic eye—"How lovely!" Emmy comments—the Maxwells leave, and Triebel (like Maxwell, like you, a William) says, "He has a diffident manner, maybe, but he's hard as nails. You have nothing to worry about with him."

I'm used to getting up at noon to start writing but that's the hour calls start arriving from people who want to talk business or stop in, and by the time I get back to work it's dark. I decide to foil the pattern with a new schedule, up at dawn, work done before lunch. The first morning I sit in a dreamlike daze and imagine I hear splashing in the pool. I go out and discover a brace of young people from the city, faces painted in psychedelic fashion, one of them Triebel's daughter, in for a swim. They're on their way to Woodstock, where a concert is scheduled. Dylan, my favorite, is supposed to perform and they figure I would want to see him. "I'd love to, any other time," I say, "but I have to work." So I miss one of the events of last century—likely for the best.

All right, I'll work in the dead of the night, I think, when no one is awake to phone or drive up, and that night I sit down at 1:00 AM, feeling the house creak around my compartment in the breakfast nook. With my first sentence an explosion of such magnitude rocks the house, I figure a car has flown off the highway and hit it broadside. I step out the back door. No cars imbedded in the house, no holes. I go through the rooms on the upper tiers, then down to the basement where I hear a hiss. I open a door to the utility room. The water heater is on its side, an explosive rip down its center, blown up—the final assault of forces intent on undoing me, as I take it, and feel that the dark gymnasium at my back, which I've never used, holds a gathering of Ben Hecht ghosts.

We pack up to live with Dad again, and on the way stop to see Care's parents in Chicago. We've hardly stepped into their apartment when the phone rings and Care's mother hands it to me. "This is Paul Newman," Newman's voice says. "You wrote *What I'm Going to Do, I Think*, right?"

"How did you know I was here?"

"I called the house number your agent gave me and your sister gave me this one. I want the film rights to your novel." Before I can explain, he says, "Yeah, I know, the guy who had Stone's *Hall of Mirrors* has your book, too. He's being a wheeler-dealer and I'm warning you, he'll screw up. I started a production company with John Foreman and we're doing *Hall of Mirrors*. I want yours for our next."

"You'll have to talk to—"

"I'm not talking to the schmuck! I want to do a film of that book and I want to play the lead!"

"Chris is only twenty-seven."

"Yeah, well, I guess I am getting old, huh, is that how you see it? Tell the kid the deal's off."

"But I have a contract with him."

"Tear it up. I can't tell you how often that's done to cut through the BS. If you want a film made, call me in a week, otherwise I guarantee you, you'll see zip. Everybody's got this guy's number and he's getting worse—the new Sam Goldwyn, he thinks! Call in a week."

When I tell Carole who it was she says, "My God!"

"He wants me to break the contract, the option I gave."

"Can you do that?" she asks.

"I don't see how you can," Dad says when we get to his place. "If you signed it, you have to live with that." I call Candida, who has a worried tone and says she'll call back, and in an hour she tells me the young man will not negotiate with Newman.

I hang up and hear Newman say, *Zip*.

12

Giving It Away

———

After a period with Dad, we return to Michigan, and one night I start to pack a group of stories I've shaved down from chapter size to their original state, mostly of the Neumiller children before they mature, ready to give up on the novel I envisioned and settle for a story collection. Care asks what I'm doing and I say I'm sending this off, this is it, I have to get a book out, and she says, "What about the earlier generations you always talked about? The burial?"

So I unpack the box and sit down and start over. I finish the piece about "Marie," not quite right, and a version of the boy running the race, a piece the *New Yorker* takes, though it seems an outline of the weighty portent that rose with a rumble that day in the wind. We move from one place to another in Michigan, and at a series of "cabins" near the lake, cement block quadrants, I sit on a cement slab that serves as the porch of one, my back against its sun-warmed block wall, and finish the proofs of "Owen's Father," which Candida sells to *Partisan Review*—a scene in the novel I thought would be my first—a story Dad said was my best, after the *New Yorker* turned it down. Or Maxwell didn't send it on.

We settle near Kewadin on an inland lake, in a cabin with no insulation, unsuited for winter, but the widow who rents it says we can stay as long as we're able to tolerate the cold (it has a heater) and the pipes don't freeze. I draft long pieces, "The End," "Home," "The History Lesson," sitting at a rickety table into the night and early morning, pursuing the Urbana novel.

One night when "Home" pushes past sixty handwritten pages and still isn't done, "The End" equally lengthy, a thought arrives as if printed across my consciousness: *Nobody will publish this.* I stand and pace the room to deal with that. I can cut my losses and settle on the collection of stories I had ready, but so much has appeared with the new pieces I have to finish them. If nothing else, I decide, I can give the typed-up book to Dad. I always meant it for him. That will be enough, I think, and sit back down and keep on.

Then it's Thanksgiving and slush is in the pipes. We buy our first new vehicle, a Jeep, with money from *What I'm Going to Do*, and add the latest innovation, a car seat of molded plastic that surrounds Newlyn's body as if she's an astronaut. Care takes the wheel and I get in our aging Bonneville convertible, packed to its fluttering canvas top with belongings and boxes of files, besides the newly drafted chapters in a fireproof safe strapped to the passenger seat, and take off, suspecting we'll end again at Dad's.

But on the way we rent a rattletrap of two rooms, with two bedrooms off them, in rural Wisconsin. The kitchen table is the only place to work, so I have to clear my pages away before every meal. I set up a schedule to work from the evening meal until sunrise, then move aside the manuscript pages and typewriter, so Carole and Newlyn can eat breakfast at the table, and I go to bed inside the scene I'm working on, dream of its people while I sleep, and rise to a waking dream of them in the exact arrangement I left them with my last sentence, the stilled unity of their interpenetrating presences and the life of the three of us turning seamless.

The characters open issues of their own, motivations and escapades that demand expansion of the pieces I thought were done, or open up whole new chapters—the twelve-page "New Year" extending beyond forty. We expect to rent the place for the winter but stay on. I begin to write poems, to sharpen my ear for prose, and a scattering of them appear in magazines and quarterlies. I realize that the opening, of the boy running a race, is the preface ("Prelude," Michael says), and I need to fill it out with passages from the present, of Tim as an adult, so I turn to that, afraid Care will say, along with Michael and others, "Aren't you done yet?" Instead she asks one winter morning whether I'm working on the piece I've talked to her about, the burial by an elderly son of his father.

I pull out the file, page through it, and with a jolt see past the scattered patches of scratching to scenes that appear as if I'm peering down a corridor at a film in progress. I've never had this experience in quite the same way. I jot down the outlines of the scenes as fast as I can, including dialogue when it comes, and then the movie dims and fades to dust.

· · ·

By spring the book is a mess, with a dozen other pieces rising from the sections I have. I list on a sheet of paper what I will and will not include, and the book I once felt I had in hand, nearly done, shifts into separate spheres. "It" is five books, I realize. I figure if I can't include them all I have the outlines of five complementary, interlocking novels, including the one I started for Maxwell, my real first novel, set aside for years, *My Brother's Visit to New York*. Maxwell asks about it still. We talk or correspond and he says there is nothing I can do when a book takes off except follow where it goes.

But your mother says, "I feel I have to kick characters out of bed or shove them aside to get in next to you."

I pull out the file folder labeled "Burial," and with a glance at a few pages see the entire story as it will stand, as if it's already written, and the experience is so unsettling, tinged with nausea, that I set the file aside. I go to the medicine chest in our narrow bathroom, which is hardly wider than my hips, and see a normal representation of me in the mirror and not a jot of the tangled inhabitants of a world of such specific dimension and weight I can hardly hold my head erect.

I pick up the ringing phone and look out at a lacework of leaves above our summer rural yard, never mowed. "Yes?"

"Larry! *Ba*-by!"

"Bob! Where are you?"

"Good news, I got the Brando role as a young guy, in Godfather II! I'm going to Sicily to study the dialect!"

"I'm not sure what 'godfather two' means but it sounds great. Congratulations."

"You haven't seen *The Godfather*?"

"Bob, we're out of it here, we're in the backwoods. I mean, we've been here a year, the outback, the boonies."

"How far did you say you're from Minneapolis? I was thinking I could stop and see you on my flight to Sicily."

"We're in the opposite direction."

"I'm in Hollywood. It'd be great to see you and Care and little New. Could you meet me at the Minneapolis airport? I got a few free days right now, before Sicily."

I look out the window and see your mother in a dazzle of light tugging at a rope to untangle it from a picketed horse, a pin-headed pinto, a foolish purchase at an auction, a horse unable to understand how to stay free of its own stakeout rope.

"Bob, there's this book I've been telling you about since I don't know when. It's overdue I forget how many years and I'm finally getting it done. Also, Care told me today, well, kind of warned me that we need to take a vacation."

"Take me along."

"I don't know. I guess we could."

"Oh," he says. And I should know that when a friend lives by a code—here, loyalty—he expects his friends to honor it, too, if they hope to remain friends, and with his "Oh" I seem to hear, as with Newman, the drawer on an antiquated cash register, the kind with push-buttons that lever mechanical numerals into a window at the top, close with a clong.

Bob says he guesses he won't see us, then, on his flight back.

Now when I sit to write, sentences arrive with such furor the typewriter not only clatters but appears to rumble under my hands. I have to leap up and pace until I quiet down. I call Maxwell and he says, "All you can do is keep at it." I begin to read the Bible to discover what the Neumiller and Jones families believed, and the Gospels, especially when Jesus is speaking, draw me in. But the next day I discover a passage that seems the opposite of the one I read the night before, and fall into unsettled confusion at keeping it straight. A presence I've sensed most of my life, which I've tried to drink or smother or mock or smoke away, hovers close, and I hear Maxwell intoning from *The Chateau,* "When you explain away one mystery, you only make room for another."

Outside, clusters of leaves glow with complexity and draw me into contemplation so intense it seems the unmown grass is about to laugh, the surface of earth racing toward its end in total dark. In that dark I harbor a secret like scrofulous mold going wild that keeps me battling to control my thoughts. The duty of the book is to uncover that secret. My bedtime is sunrise, my working nights brief, now that we've reached spring equinox, and some days I stay up past noon, using a wobbly cabinet to free the table for the two I'm writing for, besides, of course, Dad.

We start to take the Jeep to town for meals, given our limited space and the disruption of meals to my work, or I set off on long drives alone. On one trip I stop and get out and stand with my hand on a tree trunk, staring across a narrow river, and picture the elderly man in "Burial" with his hand on the same tree trunk, and feel him push off from me and walk to the river and get on his knees and plunge his head into the water and come up rubbing and shaking his hair—gray-white, I see, gray-black with the soak. What do I mean, *I see?*

I go to the water and dunk my head in to my neck, blowing

a roar of frigid bubbles, and dash to the Jeep and nearly fall out the door with the boom of an audible thought: *His brain was blank numb fragments from the bang of a sneeze.*

When I'm able to negotiate the road, I picture the pocked and dimpled peaks I saw on TV in Nyack as the first arrivals on the moon, a pair of astronauts, went bounding in silver leaps across the screen, and a reverberating thought dims my vision—*furred in fall with frost as phosphorescent as the mountainy ridges on the moon's crust*—and have to pull off on the shoulder. I look for a piece of paper. None. No pencil. I sit until I memorize the phrase, then head home.

I pull out the file "Burial" and the story falls in place so fast I'm done by morning. Thirty pages. I count them. I start typing them and hardly need to rewrite, the bang of the sneeze slipping into a sentence so determined I feel numb and fragmented, details of faces rising through that into a new focus, and when I'm finished I have thirty-five typed pages. I read the whole of it to your mother while Newlyn takes a nap, and she says, "That's it! That's what I've been waiting for!"

I drive to town and return with a case of beer and call Maxwell late that night. When his whispery voice comes on, I say, "Listen to this," and start reading the chapter. "Larry," he says. "It's two in the morning. Send it in the mail." The next day he calls and says, "You cannot do that again. You cannot call me at that hour of the night, not one time more. I forbid it. I'm an old man."

A week later, when he gets the story in the mail, he's on the phone the minute he finishes—more congratulatory and encouraging than he's been about any of my work at any other time in all the years we've worked together.

. . .

Care decides she and Newlyn *will* take a vacation, whether I am or not, and when they leave I realize the emotional edge I'm on. Sentences and phrases arrive in such echoing auditory tones I quake and can't continue. I call Michael, needing money for their vacation and a weekend visit I've decided to take to join them, and when I mention my vision of the interlocking novels, he doesn't respond to my exuberance as usual but says, "Larry, I think you need a reality check."

"How's that?"

"I mean, *maybe you're going crazy.* Will you ever finish this book?"

He ran copy for it in the Farrar, Straus catalogue for two years, then withdrew it.

We make it through the winter but I'm in collapse by spring, and we move to Minneapolis, where I enroll in an experimental program at the University Hospital. A doctor forbids me to read or write for six months, the two loves that govern my life, though to tell the truth, Joseph, the prohibition is a relief. I have an excuse not to write. Your mother and I decide I should take a position offered to me earlier by the University of Wisconsin, Madison, as writer in residence.

The contract is for one semester, but near its end the chair of the department calls me in and asks me to stay on for the rest of the year.

Care and I are standing at a pair of sliding-glass patio doors that lead to a deck where we feed raccoons, a clause in our lease, *feed the raccoons*—three dog dishes beside a pair of garbage cans—when she says she can't take it anymore. She feels

I've abandoned her. I say I'm doing all I can to hold on, I mean remain sane, for her and Newlyn's sake, in a job that settles our needs and pays off debts.

She says all I care about are my students and that damn endless book (I'm back at it in the basement), and it's true that young people are so enamored of their identities, or most are, that it's a pleasure to see them perform their paces for a watching world, as they sense it. But the teaching causes conflicts. All I've done since college is write, and I question whether my full-time editorial involvement with students, as it's become, won't compromise or soften the edge of my own work. "I haven't abandoned you," I say.

"What would you call it?"

I shove my hands in my pockets to hold them still, and remember Maxwell saying that was what he did when he didn't know what to say or how to make a decision, until enough time passed that the decision was made. He has told me he visited this campus when he was a protégé of Zona Gale and got the impression he was watching an endless musical comedy, and I feel a sudden rage at how he's defined or stepped on or stepped around or sealed off or sawed away at every shred of prose and thought I've offered him. And when Care tells me she needs help, I want to say I do, too—every time I think of my father, who's been diagnosed with cancer, and endured an operation, and now chemotherapy.

"I've stood by you all these years," she says, "and this last year was the worst. I need a spiritual connection!"

"What do you mean, 'a spiritual connection'?"

"*God*, you ass!"

Every former connection is slipping its moorings, tethers, and bolts, and any further prodding will send it downhill in an avalanche, so I feel, legs swelling with magnetic fear at the prospect. I've started seeing a shrink again, so I ask her, in the only solution that comes, if she wants to see him.

"I want you! Where are you?"

Sliding toward *timor mortis*, perhaps, though I don't fear death as much as the death of my book and Dad's death, both of which at the moment are intertwined. Just when he reached the comfortable distance of remission, the cancer returned. He has visited us twice, and from the way he avoids my eyes, staring at the floor or across the room as he talks, I know that he knows he's knocking on heaven's door.

One morning I wake to an empty bed. Carole isn't in the house. Newlyn is gone. There's no note. The night before, after a workshop, I went to a bar with a student, a Vietnam vet, and remember, hours later, dimly seeing him across the table of a booth, in a dark restaurant where I felt I was sinking through the floorboards, but can't remember how I got home.

The dresser is bare. Its upper drawers, Care's, are empty, as I find in quick pulls. The leather suitcase I gave her at Christmas, an unfounded extravagance, she said, is not in her closet. The nearly matching suitcase she gave me, an extravagance she said I deserved, neither of us knowing what the other bought, as if enacting a version of O. Henry with signals that were identical but working at cross-purposes—stands instead where hers once stood. Our car is in the drive. Most of the clothes are gone from Newlyn's room and a leather bank bag packed with pocket change is missing.

The difficulty with me, I know, now with drink added, is *IT*—her term for the book our lives have circled for a decade. I told her a dozen times it was done, which she saw as promises, and took the *final* final draft to New York over Christmas break and went through it with Michael in his apartment. He would read a sentence and pause, giving me time to decide whether it was on target or I could fix or exclude it, and we went over every sentence of the 800-page manuscript that way. Two weeks. When I got back Care said, "Well?"

I couldn't look at her, and felt I could never look at the book again. "Michael wants me to work on a few chapters."

"What?"

Now it's May, with student stories to finish editing for final grades, and I know it's my lack of resolution about *IT* that sent her off. I call the police. They say they'll do what they can but assure me the situation isn't unusual.

"I'm sure she'll call soon," a detective tells me.

She calls the next night and says she wants me to know that she and Newlyn are safe and well where they are, but won't say where that is. I ask what I should do about the house, since our lease on it ends in a month, and she says she doesn't care. That's not like her. She doesn't want to talk, she says. She'll write. I have the call traced and find it originates in the Chicago suburb where her parents live.

Dad helps me move out and pack everything the three of us accumulated at Madison in a storage shed he assembled a year ago to hold our other belongings. I keep my manuscript and financial records and rent an apartment in Madison, planning to finish the novel there. But when I run out of money in the fall I move in with him again. I arrange books and mementos, "mnemonic devices," I call them, in his basement, and at its center set up our bed from Brooklyn Heights. It occurs to me that Newlyn, now six, was conceived where I lie as if flung aside, hoping to sleep to the end of the sleeplessness that opens my book and the years of sleeplessness it's caused.

Before any reconciliation can come, I have to finish *IT,* I understand, so I get out the manuscript and sit at a rolltop desk similar to one described in the novel—a desk Dad saved from destruction at a public school. I imagine myself an editor more ruthless than any I've encountered and cut phrases, sentences, paragraphs, pages, narrowing every scene, and the more I cut the more I find I can. In the process, I begin to learn from the characters, a kind of comeuppance.

They veer from my confines, which I thought were as fixed as the steppes of stars, parade-drilled, whole ranks wavering off as I see each character anew and see that he or she carries ideas different from mine, and that the divisions in families and the disunities in marriage are the result of religion, or lack of it. Why my surprise, when the generative focus of the book, from the first Neumiller story on, was the spiritual state of its people? That was the concern Carole was trying to communicate, I see in retrospect, and we did attend a campus Catholic chapel, with guitars for music and bread loaves passed around at communion, and afterward she would say with a hopeful look, "Well, what did you think?"

To my Tridentine background the service was turned around backward, literally, too informal, but with a new attraction: the readings from the Gospels and Epistles that connected with memories as familiar as the well-worn walk to my work desk. But I felt bricked in, Poe's Fortunato, by skepticism, mistrust, misgivings—the superiority of dismissal I adopted to show I was hip, while behind the bricks a rage kept up at all that had gone wrong from my mother's death to the mental smashup of last year—trying to finish a book that seemed destined not to be, besides a growing disbelief that any good could come from any dedicated work, self gone in a wisp, while religion claimed it was only from such acts that good was wrung.

Michael calls to find out how I'm doing, and when I hang up Dad is hovering close, anxious for news. "Michael says he'd like to meet you," I say, as indeed he has.

"That's nice to hear. I'd certainly like to meet him."

I have two quarts of pennies, my only funds, my meals on Dad, and late at night when work is done I walk a mile to a roadhouse on the highway where I can get draft beer for twenty cents a glass. One night when I sit at the rolltop desk, the body of the manuscript parts and turns sexual, shining parts linked to parts below, and I understand that every decision of every character is overseen by a sexual, spiritual outlook.

No matter what a character claims as his religion, or when one says he has none, as some do, his acts are governed by belief—from the cars some drive to the clothes they wear and the jobs they take and the reasons they give for that. If there isn't unity in belief or belief diverges in a marriage, both sides have trouble making sense and start disagreeing on everything the other brings up.

But what seems relevant is how Care, the forerunner in our relationship, was true to her instincts ("*God*, you ass!") and drew me after, as she was drawn when I was reading the Bible and wrote "Burial." I sense a slice of hope might exist for us to incline in agreement, if we can begin to agree on the IT above the *IT* of the book, and then Dad walks up and says, "Would you want to go to a retreat house with me?"

. . .

It's one of the places where he works as custodian and fixit man, as his health holds. I tell him I can't afford any fee, and he says he's fixed that; if I'll write a piece describing the retreat house, that will serve as payment. That same day I receive the galleys of *Beyond the Bedroom Wall*, finally, which I show him when they arrive, and then remind him I have to finish corrections right away. "Take them along," he says.

Whoever I am is scattered through the *IT* it's taken ten years to get to galleys, and I'm geographically scattered, too, over every place I sat to write, now that I'm drawing the chapters, each with a separate external aura, to a close, as if locations, too, are being sealed off. I imagine death as a similar stepping down to levels of loss, but death is an end, not the continuing dispersal I'm contending with. I can contain the dispersal enough to keep essentials of me from flying off, my muscles joining in the containment in aching tension, and I'm able to sit in a chair and write in longhand, if I form the letters slowly, and that's it. I'm not sure I can keep that up if I'm alone. So I leave with Dad.

I sit in a reading room and realize I'm staring at the spine of *Seven Storey Mountain*, a book I always intended to read. I pick it up but can't get past the first paragraph, the path from my eyes to my mind sealed. I'm not sure how soon the management wants my description, so with trembling hands I write, "Near Rockford, Illinois, not far from the Rock River, in a placid setting surrounded on all sides by low hills covered by hardwoods, is the Bishop Lane Retreat House."

I don't believe I can go on, but a first sentence is no more than belief, unless one does. "A small stream, winding down from the hills, forms a pond a few hundred feet from the front door." The prose of PR. I go to my room but can't rest. I switch on a desk lamp and pick up the galleys where I left off. Dad comes into the room and paces, and then stands at my elbow and asks me how long I can keep this up.

I'm not sure what he means, not sure how to answer, so I hand him a sheaf of floppy galleys, two feet long, and he goes to his room across the hall. I'm hardly done with the next galley sheet when he returns. He says it's good, very good, he likes it. "But these little changes, you know, don't you feel you're picking flyshit out of pepper?" A flare of anger? "I think you need a break. Come and help me in the kitchen."

We go to the dining room by a door other than the usual one and I feel confused, as if the corridors of schools and hospitals and now, retreat houses, are connected to a network of illness, so you need a guide to find the door to get you out—back at the sink with him as a boy. The group on retreat is finishing dinner, and Dad shows me how to spray the dishes stacked in one sink and set them in a rack inside another. The rack glides into a dishwasher that sends billowing steam out its bottom. The people finishing dinner come one by one toward the counter I stand behind until too many are staring through me, and then they disperse into a fog like the steam, a clouded mass, their eyes lit with the energy of an otherworld, and a ruby-eyed old man rumbles, "God bless you, son."

I take his tray, and the misty group shudders toward me, the only solidity their eyes, the force field of them traveling through me in a whine, and I feel for my face as it lifts off in a molecular rush, vaporous as the cloudy mass of them mingling with me until I'm whisked off in a transport I want to end so I don't fall too far.

·   ·   ·

"Yes, it happens," somebody says. "It's happened here before."
A nun, I think, says it, as the person supporting me goes staggering past. Dad holds one of my arms over the back of his neck, his other hand around my waist, and helps me down a hall where I see the galleys of the novel under a lamp on a desk go past, and then I notice I have on his slippers.

How did they get on my feet?

"Are you better now?" he asks. "I think you fainted."

He takes me to my room, lowers me onto the bed, swings my feet up on it, pulls his slippers off, and I want to ask how they got there—but he presses me down and says, "You're overworked, Larry. Get some rest." And with that I'm asleep.

We stay for two weeks, I work on a description of the retreat house when the galleys are too much, and then it's time to leave for New York. The galleys are off, taken before I finish corrections by a book club, although Michael wants me to go over three chapters in manuscript, to see if I can shorten them, and these he'll have the printer pour into the page proofs being set up as I finish them. Candida offers her apartment, since she won't be in the city for a couple of weeks, and I bend to this final task, or this final task yet once more: "The Village Poet," easy after I find a new first sentence, "Home," and "New Year."

I cut fifteen pages.

I gave over the physical tie to my parents at thirty-four, Joseph, the age my mother was when she died, and my age when my father died. You've been a helicopter pilot for two years, and when you left the farm I gave you over, too, in a sense— to the unquiet world, anyway—and as you've aged into the person you are I understand I'll have to give you over, as a father

must, in the ultimate sense. I think of the hundreds of accident-
and incident-free hours you've flown, and wonder if that doesn't
place you in a category where— And now you've sent an e-mail
giving your approximate location in Iraq—

And I know I have to stop this, give you over indeed, and
with that thought I sense an accompanying ugly aridity as
though you have died, or I have, in order to give you over,
which I must do to allow you to pursue a selfhood independent
of mine—indeed of both your mother and me.

The last snow lies on the buttes to the south in flat rounds
like banquet plates, and as I take in a dose of the reflected brilliance—a granular haze gripping the land in a frieze of stilled
perfection—my thoughts move off from the body in my arms,
her, the one who returned to give birth to you two years later,
and settle on you, as I now know the thoughts and prayers of
my father settled on me at the beginning and all of the way
through my up-and-down interims until his last step broke
through the membranous reality we know as life and came
down hard on that eternal reality that takes the best and worst
of us for good, death.

13

Nutshell Kingdom

———

"Oh, God, I could be bounded in a nutshell and count myself a king of infinite space," Hamlet says to his false friends from the university, "were it not that I have bad dreams." And, oh, Joseph, I've survived being bound in opposed phases, especially this last with the PTO, but my bad dreams still recur. And I don't mean dreams sprung by sleep, as Hamlet did not, but my waking concern for you and others younger, and the manner of your education—its lacks and disruptions to the integrity of learning, best illustrated by the universal educator, babysitter, and tutor, TV.

It's not only TV, any more than it's video games or plugs in the ears or cell phone calls in cars or between classes; it's the manner of education you receive, with television a mirror of its goals, so that you said after your first year of college, "I did fairly well, but what I really learned was how to play pool and improve on my game of ping-pong."

I won't say, as Maxwell might, "Whatever possessed you!" because I know the discouragement education can be.

So sing to me, Muse, of the 1970s, when I was writer in residence at the University of Wisconsin, and found that my fiction workshop was the only creative writing course on the campus, unlike the sophisticated system I experienced at the University of Illinois. There I learned that time worships language, as Auden says; time gets down on its knees to words, Joseph, as time is whisked away in the words I set down here for you, which outlive me. Even when writing is tinged by the term "creative," it's practical; it sets us in its time.

The English Department at Madison held a party to welcome new faculty members before classes began, with a bounty of wine and Wisconsin beer, and of the seventy faculty members present a junior fellow came up and said, "I didn't want you here. I wanted Paul Theroux." And turned and walked off.

I have favorite writers, too, and like to see passion for writers, but that's no way to treat a stranger. All writers have favorites, but they're aware of the difficulties that come to those who publish more than one book (for some, one is enough), and this was my first glimpse of the Cyclops or uni-view and the rude dogmatism that has captured universities since—the opposite of the latitude of study and consideration I encountered at the University of Illinois and in the variety of artists your mother and I befriended in New York.

My contract was for the fall semester, but the chair asked me to stay on, and close to Christmas the first chapter of *Beyond the Bedroom Wall*, "Burial," appeared. Maxwell still spoke of it with affection, and I assumed a *New Yorker* story would raise collegial interest—not a bid for attention; it was my eighteenth story to appear in the magazine.

I knew most of the faculty subscribed to the *New Yorker*, because I saw it every week in the wall of departmental mailboxes, not to mention issues on desktops and *New Yorker* cartoons posted on walls and doors. The week the story appeared, nobody said a word. None of the faculty mentioned it. Weeks later, as I stood staring at the issue carrying the story on the desk of the assistant to the chair, she said she enjoyed my "article." So I figured it was in the issues the rest received and I wasn't caught in a Kafkaesque mirage, as it sometimes felt, walking the echoing concrete corridors—an entire building the home of the English department.

Graduate assistants, the oarsmen of any university ship, required to teach literacy to undergraduates, would ask "Have you read *Gravity's Rainbow*?" and questions of the kind, but the faculty seldom talked about books, which gives an idea of my naiveté; I assumed English professors were interested in writing. I called Maxwell and he said, "That may be typical of English departments nowadays."

An incident from the present registers the route of English departments since. A graduate student I've worked with at a university a thousand miles from Madison said in a recent phone call, "You know, it's amazing, but it looks like I'll graduate with a master's degree in English literature without taking one course in English lit. Hardly any are offered, and none this semester!" It was his last.

All his courses were in theory or in methods of teaching theory, besides writing workshops. He called later to say that one of the faculty had returned from a sabbatical in Europe and would be teaching the only lit course offered in the department his final semester, on one novel, *Ulysses*.

If Maxwell mentioned a book I would get it and, if I liked it, read all I could find of that writer. On some visits to his office he had a book waiting; I took it and read it and we talked about it on the next visit. Two or three times he hurried me into the elevator, took me down to a shop around the corner, and bought a book and handed it to me: *imperative*.

I've taught at a dozen colleges and universities in different areas of the country, sometimes for a semester or two, a summer, a year and a half, five years in the East, at the congenial post you received with less enthusiasm, Joseph; for a semester in London and, later, a summer seminar at Cambridge, and I've helped organize two schools, drawing on Dad's experience, so I've seen education from a variety of angles. That's why I have bad dreams. I've seen the views of university faculties narrow until they're closed to every idea they don't endorse. Those they do endorse are culturally popular and religious-political, because politics is the fire-breathing fundamentalism of the university. This is death to rational thought.

Ruth R. Wisse, a Harvard professor, wrote in a recent piece for the *Wall Street Journal*, "The Federal Election Commission could not have foreseen that when it required employment information on political donations of over $200, it would expose scandalous uniformity in a university community that advertises its diversity. The *Sacramento Bee* reported that the University of California system gave more to the Kerry campaign than any other single employee group, and that Harvard was second, with only 15,000 employees to UC's 160,000."

Wisse then lists the percentage of donations to Kerry at other colleges, compared to those for Bush: Cornell, 93 percent, Dartmouth, 97 percent, Yale, 93 percent.

In a syndicated column George Will noted that, according to "the nonpartisan Center for Responsive Politics," of "the top five institutions in terms of per capita contributions to presidential candidates, the third, fourth and fifth were Time Warner, Goldman Sachs and Microsoft. The top two were the University of California system and Harvard, both of which gave about 19 times more money to John Kerry than to George Bush."

The point is not the outlook of this or that political party but the uniformity within a closed system.

In her article Wisse adds that students at Harvard "making the transition from liberal to conservative"—or those who begin to resist the prevailing view—"are often wounded by their first exposure to the contempt that greets their support for the war in Iraq or opposition to abortion or whatever else separates them from the liberal campus." The separation is so hostile as it arrives from the majority of professors that many students, seeking approval or better grades, cave in.

And not only students, as Wisse notes: "A junior professor told me that when she began teaching at Harvard she resigned from several organizations that would have betrayed her conservative leanings. She hadn't wanted to give colleagues an easy excuse for voting her down when she came up for tenure; but now that the prospect of tenure was before her, she didn't know whether she wanted to stay on in such a repressive community."

An estimate based on these and other statistics, such as voting records, suggests that 3 percent of tenured faculty in

America hold views contrary to the uni-view. Hold whatever view you wish, despise a candidate or a war, even if it doesn't touch on you personally, or criticize the way an officeholder fumbles for words (though I've received faculty memos one wouldn't want a proofreader to check), as long as you don't hold that over the heads of students and drill it into them daily, but allow the latitude of a diversified view.

I've attended departmental business meetings that turn into political rallies, with cheers for the good guy and bashing of the other, while items on the docket stand idle. The assumption of such behavior is that the consensus is universal and that a state school bears no responsibility to its supporters, the taxpayers. A bright graduate student I know who disagreed with a professor received a final grade of C, which is failing in grad school. When he complained, the instructor raised it to a B and sent a note saying, "If I had known this was the kind of student you would be, I wouldn't have written you such a good recommendation for grad school."

I like equipoise. I prefer balance and reasoned talk to polemics. I hope to achieve balance among my variety of fictional characters. I do balancing exercises. I enjoy the feel of my body in harmony with the relationships between plants and creatures and all forms of life that sustain our precarious balance. The human presence is the balancing agent, and if you attend only to animals or pets, forage dies. Every growing entity needs a helping hand, whether to set the seedling or sow the grain or deal with predators or weeds or prune or graft or remove the dead and heal the diseased.

One day, in the aftermath of a minor breakdown, I went to Maxwell for advice; Frances Steloff, a well-known mid-city bookseller of moderns, was offering her entire collection of Dylan Thomas for a thousand dollars, a hefty sum in 1966.

"Are you sure you want to spend that much on his books?" Maxwell asked, aware that I'd recently acquired a set of antique Britannica at the Scribner bookstore on Fifth.

"I think so." My affection for Thomas dated from college, when I listened to him read his poetry and the poems of others on Caedmon recordings from the library, and some of those LPs, too, were included in the Steloff collection.

Maxwell swiveled his chair to look out at the sky, and in my state I imagined him thinking how it would feel to make the money I had at my age by writing. He raised his hands and locked them behind his head, as he did when he was pleased, and swiveled back to me. "Why not, if you're going to enjoy having these," he said. "Maybe it's a gift ordained."

We both laughed. I was only a week out of the hospital and would have trusted him with my life. I mentioned that I bargained a bit and had the price down a hundred dollars. "It's the first time I've done that."

"No," he said. "You did that with the guitar."

He meant a guitar I bought after I met him, when my first was stolen, and I told him how I finagled a pawnshop dealer down a few dollars. What kind of memory did he have? I would have to watch it, as they say. But I bought the Thomas.

"You must draft a story in one sitting," he said more than once. "At least get the gist of it down in a sitting. And then spend no more than a month getting it right. If it doesn't work by then it likely won't."

He took me for lunch to the Century Club and to Luchows where, in the era before cell phones, a waiter walked through the restaurant with a slate signboard hanging from his neck and rang a recess bell to alert patrons to phone calls—their names and the numbers to call chalked on the board. "A bit of exhibitionism," Maxwell said. He ordered shad roe during their running season, and as appetizer for us both a plate of bluestem oysters. He took me on picnics to Central Park, to the Coin d'Paris and specialty restaurants he must have seen as necessary to my education and got the bill himself, or so I suspect, since he paid cash. He took me to MOMA more than once, paying my admission, and I'm not sure he led me to Giacometti's "Palace at 4 AM," a central image from *So Long, See You Tomorrow,* but I remember staring up at the bronze of Balzac in the sculpture garden and hearing sonorous music. After hours of wandering hallways and galleries, or the hobble-legged spiral of the Guggenheim, he would sit on a bench and say, "I think we'd better leave, if you're suffering as much as I from museum fatigue."

For students who aspire to a similar liberal education, which used to mean a liberal application of study in the humanities from a variety of perspectives, it would be best to enroll in a private college, perhaps one established by a Christian organization or church. In most of these the imperative for inclusiveness and liberality is preserved.

Some of the small private schools aspire to mirror the Ivies or become a kind of evangelical Yale, and they may not be the best. The origins of Yale are, of course, evangelical. It was established by Puritans, along with Harvard and Princeton and other ivied institutions that were, at first, divinity schools. So the Christian tag is not an imprimatur for a diversified education.

At a smaller institution of Christian orientation or independent status or both, the faculty get to know one another and may eat together at a common or high table in the Oxbridge manner, as I've seen at a small independent school in North Dakota, Jamestown College. The faculty conversation at midday meals promotes intellectual scrutiny and provides a crosspollination that adds depth to the context of knowledge of each professor.

Specialization in such an atmosphere is augmented by breadth. The Jamestown faculty tend to hold degrees from esteemed institutions (from a past less homogenized) but are underpaid on a national scale—united in their vision to ensure a superior education for their students. "It's a *vocation*," an esteemed and widely published professor at the college recently said, one who had studied to be a priest and to whom "vocation" meant a spiritual calling.

There are bright spots in the monad world of the uni-view. I've worked with students in the past year who are as sharp as any since the 1970s, and they don't seem exceptions. The astute teacher Charles Johnson, a writer honored for his essays and novels of the African American experience, said of recent classes at the University of Washington, Seattle, "I'm coming across more young students who are readers. This is encouraging."

At a university writer's conference in 2005, Johnson was an honored guest, along with Marilyn Nelson, the poet laureate of Connecticut, also an African American, and the two were part of a panel that included a host and a young songwriter from Brooklyn. An audience of perhaps two hundred assembled to hear the panel, and at one point the discussion moved to critics and critical theory and Johnson, who holds a Ph.D. in philosophy and has published a book of critical prose and another on the practice of Buddhism, said, "I never bought into deconstruction."

The host, perhaps hoping to keep matters light, said, "I never even bought the book." There was laughter, a scattering of applause, and the chair of the English Department, the sponsor of the event, rose up and said with enough force for those in the area to hear, "Those arrogant, self-indulgent *bastards!*" and walked out. Her reaction may seem out of bounds, considering the guests, but represented departmental verity, where theory is king.

What embroils the academy are the examples of enduring art that exist in texts and how, at the center of most, is THE TEXT in whose wake the tradition of Western literature has carried on for centuries: the Bible. Its text accepts all genders and classes and races and refutes the fundamentalism of politics, which is exclusionary.

Those whose minds are set to resist the text (experienced by readers as a further reality) that other generations have battled over or battered against, or have seen as so porous as to suggest a being so far removed from human imagination its reaches are infinite. Many of the noisiest critics of the Bible haven't read it, or not much of it, as they would not presume to do with Homer or Shakespeare or Jane Austen. They've heard stories about it or seen others acting in opposition to its ethics, and that's it.

A good number of courses could explore the references to stories or statements from the Bible used by writers from the Beowulf poet and Chaucer and Shakespeare to Flannery O'Connor and Marilynne Robinson and Susan Howatch. In many classes on moderns, undergraduates encounter instead the borderline or off-the-chart antics of the second-rate and precious, these often sinking into sentimental and self-indulgent nihilism or existential boo-hooing alien to the dignity of Camus.

At a university where I taught, a committee was formed to establish a university press, and along with the press courses that would deal with the business of publishing: editing, proof-reading, production, and the like. I attended the meetings, and the first two dealt with the type of grants that might be available. Nobody had assembled a list of available grants—it was whatever popped up as people talked.

At the third meeting the chair appointed a young faculty member to bring to the next meeting research on universities with established presses that were teaching courses of the kind they wanted to establish. I assumed this faculty member, a new hire, was from a university where a system of the sort was set up. Instead, we received two printouts with the explanation, "That's all I could find on the Internet."

I've guided a dozen books from the first sentence through galleys and page proofs down the phases of production, during a time when publishers allowed authors to take an active part in that, asking for their opinion on page design and typography, dust jacket art, flap copy, and the rest, so I offered to teach one of the courses. The chair of the committee, who was already scheduled for a "practicum" on academic editing, said, "I might ask you to *visit*." This meant I didn't have a Ph.D.

A faculty member I admired in the East, a wise charmer who was on most of the important academic committees and also served as chair of the county Democratic Committee, appeared in my office after a similar unbusinesslike episode at a departmental meeting, and said, "These academic professionals, as they're called." He shook his head. "They have so few practical skills and such an appalling lack of knowledge about the way the real world works, it's a wonder they know how to tie their own shoes."

The discussions about a university press took place four years ago, and the department is still talking about it.

Literary art does not serve a system, or even itself. It serves another or, as Willa Cather might say, *The Other*, down on its knees. The education I received from Maxwell over a decade was vindicated in one practical stroke by a writer. In the period between reducing by fifteen pages the last three chapters of *Beyond the Bedroom Wall* and the appearance of bound books, I hung around the halls of Farrar, Straus like a homeless person on a search for a cardboard box in which to settle myself and my decade of words. The books at last arrived, with their mystical scent of glue and ink, and I sent inscribed copies to all who had helped or encouraged me along the way—those whose addresses I still had after ten years.

And then the most trying time of any book, the blank doldrums as you wait for the first review, which, as a fellow writer described, feels like dropping a rock down a well and listening on and on to hear its splash. Whenever I met or passed my editor Michael in the halls, he would say, "Don't you have someplace you should be? Someplace to go?" or "Shouldn't you find something to do? Like write a book?"

During one of the most depressing lows of that depressing interim I was perched on the edge of a wastebasket, as if I belonged in it, while I talked to a young publicist, feeling myself sink deeper, when Roger Senior, president of Farrar, Straus, rushed in with a large tear sheet in his hands and said, "I persuaded one of my spies at the *Times* to smuggle this out for me, after she told me the review was headed for the front page, but this was all she could get away with."

I tried to stand, the wastebasket clinging to my butt, and after extricating myself to Roger's "Good God!" I leaned over the sheet on the publicist's desk that the three of us were trying to get our heads around to read. It was by John Gardner, and in a long introduction he spoke about the dearth of long novels in our day, and how he told a friend the next breakthrough would be a copious novel readers would laugh and weep their way through (So what are you saying about *mine*, I thought), and in the last sentence of the smuggled-in sheet he turned to my novel and wrote, "It seems to me that nothing more beautiful and moving has been written in years."

That was my vindication; that was enough.

The practical application of education to the lives of young people has all but vanished, Joseph, and that's another facet to the grandfather you wanted to know; he retired early because he believed that to exalt a salary, as he felt his union was doing, to the detriment of the quality of teaching, was not compatible with his view of the profession. He retired in 1972, three years before I stood over the tear sheet of that review in New York City.

On a recent Christmas visit, before you left for Iraq, you spent most of your time attending to details I had let slide—wiring in new lights and switches for your mother, soldering in copper fittings and shutoffs to a sink that needed new faucets and another I decided to replace. The one that needed fixing dated from the 1950s, set in a wall of the mud room, as the Berns called it, and I couldn't find a match for its ancient horizontal faucets, so I cut a piece of cedar to cover the hole left by their bulky contrivance, and hoped to attach a new set to it.

"I'm not sure this is going to work," I said.

"Oh, Dad," you said, "you can fix anything!"

My impression is I dropped everything into the sink as I turned to you. "No," I said. "That's you. *You're* the one who can fix anything."

"No," you said, and stared straight at me, not about to give, and added, "I learned it from you," echoing a passage in my first memoir, which you proofread, when our neighbor Kenny says about a son who did so well at Sony that executives asked him where he got his expertise, he answered, "From my dad on our farm in North Dakota." And I can't tell whether you've said what you have on purpose. I know that as Maxwell had to prove himself before he could bend back around to forgive his father, so it's taken me a series of internal contortions to forgive myself for the injuries I caused you. You've recovered enough to fly a helicopter, however, which takes full coordination of all four limbs, plus balance and derring-do, the most difficult maneuver hovering in place, as you've said. I wanted to take you in my arms but the Slavic German nobility seldom stoops to such demonstrations, although we've learned to embrace each other in outpourings of affection, as if generations from my father's side have joined in our embrace.

So I hovered as you hover, and then it was time to eat.

Here in the present, in the downslide and upgrade since the PTO, I walk over ground the freeze has gripped and then let go, gripped and let go, and on my walks encounter mounds of manure left by the horses when we confined them to the three acres of our yard in the fall, to give the pasture a rest. I let fly at the mounds with my boot, scattering their richness, and realize I've become, in a literal sense, what my Chicago friends at the University of Illinois used to call everybody who came from downstate: a shit-kicker. But the skill is handy if you plan to negotiate the kingdom of organized education.

The teaching you receive from those involved in actual work is best, Joseph, which is what I got from Maxwell. The last time I saw him in his office, as he was nearing the magazine's arbitrary retirement age, seventy, two young editors were occupying separate chairs—one at the table where Maxwell worked with me on galleys, the other at a sort of student's desk beside his couch, as if his editorship couldn't be contained and had split into the sensitive young man who lost his mother and the hard-nosed editor from New York. By then he had read most of the galleys I delivered to him earlier, and said, "Tell your editor Michael he's brilliant, an artist. It's really something, what you two have done."

He was not an ungenerous, self-indulgent artiste.

That wasn't his last word, and in the decades from that time to his death, most of what he had to say was educational and encouraging, as when I at last repaid a loan he made to us during a lean spell, so we had heat one winter: "You're the only writer who's paid me back with interest."

And at a time when I was feeling discouraged enough to wonder whether it was worth going on, he called and said, "You're the only writer I know who's gone off and lived his convictions, not just put them in writing."

. . .

A while ago I was in the midst of a search through my office for a page or paragraph I couldn't find, a situation that occurs more often now, when a letter from Maxwell that I photocopied for somebody and then decided not to send—its first half too congratulatory to my cause—fell from a file. I skipped to its last half, able to appreciate more fully his story as I calculated he was eighty-nine at the time when he wrote it, and had taken the train alone to New York City from his summer house on Baptist Church Road in hot August, in order to pay tribute to a lifelong friend, Robert Fitzgerald, the incomparable translator of the *Iliad* and the *Odyssey*—long after Fitzgerald's death—in a manner Maxwell best describes, in the breathtaking panache of instantaneous composition:

Last Tuesday I was in the city to have my teeth cleaned and to see an exhibition of paintings by Robert Fitzgerald's son Barnaby. I was surprised when I emerged from the gallery to find there was a heavy rainstorm going on. Which means, of course, no taxis and I had to get to Grand Central. While I was wondering what to do, the light on top of a stationary taxi flashed on, and I rushed out into the rain to get it. The door opened and a young man tried to open his umbrella before stepping out into the rain. He saw me standing there and said, "It's a good thing for you that I'm a friend of Salander O'Reily" (the gallery owner) and as I was saying to him how indebted I was to him for providing me with a taxi a young woman appeared out of nowhere and insinuating herself between us got into the cab. Whereupon the young man said, "No, you can't do that. It's his taxi," and she got out. Imagine. On the way to Grand Central, at about 59th Street, on Park Avenue, the cloudburst turned into a hailstorm. Shortly after that the motor of the taxi stalled, and wouldn't start through three or four changes of the lights, so I got out, stepped under a marquee, and tried to adjust to the idea of a long walk to Grand Central, when I looked up the street and there was another taxi with his light on. The doorman had a lot of people under the marquee waiting for him to get a cab for them but I was more motivated and shot out into the traffic and nailed it, and made my train with two minutes to spare. With, also, a sense that angels had been taking care of me.

When I was in my twenties Zona Gale [the mentor to Maxwell in Wisconsin] said that I was a harmonious being. Pleased with the remark, I repeated it to Fitzgerald, who said, "Be careful when you are crossing the street." But if angels weren't watching over me, one old and decrepit man in the rain, who was?

14

In Another Place

———

Time to take off in the escape mode of America, with no regard
for a two-day snow. It was on drives like this, alone, Joseph,
that I learned what it's like to grow old, or saw one route age
takes, and once we're down our lane and onto the gravel I'll say
how. Oh, the clutch on this Bronco is shot and the body has the
bone-rattling sway over washboard roads of a pinheaded horse
too dumb to buck, *so if you can hear me above it all*, I'll tell you
what I haven't told anybody else.

First in jerky preface: I know you figure I drive with half my
mind, which isn't much, when we only use, as I've read somewhere, 10 percent, so I'll stay alert.

Next in shame: when I was in my fifties and climbed into our
pale yellow station wagon to drive to town at night, some sort
of slippage set me on a road I used to drive forty years ago—one

that was a thousand miles off. It was my first glimpse of the overstuffed state of my mind, filled not only with people I know or have met and characters from my books and the thousand others shelved around the house, but the varieties of nature, its geography and wildlife and weather at the scores of places we've lived, besides an inner mechanical maze of the machinery you and I have repaired over the years.

This jam-packed state, along with a growing mistrust in the nerves that parcel out details so I can manage it all, made me imagine when I looked out the windshield like this, sorry, at a solitary tree on the plain, that I was seeing a tree on the plain of Serengeti; then its branches would take on the appearance of Beethoven in profile or some similar great.

Once when I was coming back from town, down the hill to the bridge, I caught a flash of sun off metal—a Piper Cub gliding toward me on a collision course. I hit the brakes, sliding all over, and in the altered angle saw that the Piper's wings were the tinned peak of the abandoned house on the hill I've seen so many times I no longer see it, with the chimney at its center serving as a blurred propeller. Hunters from out of state bought the property and burned the house down last month, so that illusion won't recur.

Another time I was coming down the hill at a good clip when a bag from a pastry I bought in town caught a draft from the wind wing and slid toward me in such a familiar way I reached for the cat that used to patter across the seat and dive in my lap, pouring purring into my pants—dead for a year. Too much stored upstairs.

What I couldn't control was the road becoming the road I used to drive forty years ago. That road was in Illinois. Our station wagon would sway and jolt at the same places Dad's car

did on the Illinois road—the center line under my lights turning to a blur as I started into the curve outside town and saw a
grove of Illinois trees rush at me from the roadside, just as they
did when I was sixteen.

I hit the brakes and pulled onto the shoulder, telling myself
I was on Highway 21 in North Dakota, and cranked my head
around the way Dad did when he was trying to get his bearings.
I felt my mind was at the bottom of the groove of one of my
ancient LPs, stuck there. Ambushes of age are worse the first
time around, Joseph. You get used to them.

I'll pause for the stop sign at the highway instead of continuing on, as I usually do, to keep rolling—hardly ever any
traffic—because I don't want this Bronco going into a slide, and
I'm heading east, not west. West is the direction I was always
tending when the road turned into another.

It was an Illinois blacktop like this and it ran from the town
where we lived to the next, five miles off, and every time it rose
through Highway 21 I could picture the main street ahead as if
seeing it in a movie—that gift and curse I have to control when
I drive. I realized the road was one-half of the run I made most
every Saturday night to visit the girl I was dating, one I coyly
called *Inamorata* in a poem I got printed in a local newspaper,
hoping to impress her.

But here's the crest of Bentley Hill, where you get a view
of the lay of the land, lying in such still rolls it seems ocean
waves have paused here to rest, the buttes and plateaus like
thoughts rising from a mind sunk in sleep. On my side it looks
like a sow the size of a city has thrown herself on her back for
display—all those nipples and cones dotting the hills. These
ditches produce our best yucca. That windmill was transplanted
from a ranch surely smothered under this snow. Imagine all the

empty houses and barns and sheds across the countryside, and then imagine the silence of the spaces between them that nothing enters, other than snow and rain and wildlife, stretches no human being has walked, and you get a sense of the stillness natives experienced.

The associations I carry after fifty can be a help, if I can locate *that* one at the bottom of the LP groove when I need it, or they consume so much of my attention in their demands they tend to pull reality apart—that rattling deconstruction, noisy as this Bronco, known as going mad.

An insight came one night when I was driving whichever road it was, but it took a death to do it.

It was the year I decided to quit smoking and made it all through summer, but one October night I went sneaking off in the station wagon, headlights blank until I was over the hill, and by the time I reached the highway I was shivering so badly I had to turn on the heater. It gave off a stench of mouse piss, a hidden nest, and I felt a presence behind, too large for a rodent—a cat, I thought, one of the seven on the farm. But it came closer, taking the shape of a man, and I swung around, my hair giving off the electricity it does when I fear for my life, and I saw that the backseat, the space between seats, the cargo space—everything was bare.

When I got my swerving back under control the presence leaned near my neck, and my first thought was, *It's Satan!* I was too intelligent, though, to give in to delusion, right, and filed that away as another symptom of age. But on the way back, with a cigarette in my mouth that tasted like tar, the presence swung into place at the same spot and a shape leaped from a tree row. It paused on the shoulder, a deer frozen in the headlights, and I knew at the sight I was going to hit it.

I got to the brake but was going so fast inertia tripped the two-ton wagon with its 400-horsepower engine into a skid, the rear end sliding around as if it meant to pass the engine, and as I got even with the deer in a growling slide—a doe, I saw—she leaped. I couldn't have been doing more than thirty at the moment, because in the next second I was stopped, but the impact sent the deer skidding away up the road on her flank. She bounced into the air at the opposite shoulder, legs flying up with a rubbery look, and slid into the ditch.

A shriek spread from the car. It was the radiator, spraying steam through a rip that squealed, as I found in a quick check, and then got back in and raced home before the engine overheated, in the jumpy confusion that overtakes me when I've done something "harebrained," as Dad put it. I ran for the house to call the sheriff, to report the dead deer, and remembered that when I drove the Illinois road that kept rising through this one, it was in his car, the first new car we owned—or, as I said when I pulled up to somebody to offer a ride, removing a cigarette from my ear where I stored it like a pencil and letting it dangle from my lips as I hit the lighter, "It's Dad's car."

The night of the deer, Dad had been dead a dozen years, and when I sneaked off to town the next time I realized he was the presence at my ear. He wanted me to quit smoking, stick to my resolve, preserve my health for your sakes, as I received it, for as long as I could.

So. It wasn't that the roads were that similar; it was my state of mind. In my Illinois past I drove with longing toward a young woman with love on my mind, and in the present my love for you in the waiting house, all of you, was at an adolescent height, now that we were back from the East, and with that thought the road switched back to the real one.

This is the story I haven't told.

. . .

Fathers and sons bond—if I may call it that—in cars. The car I drove in Illinois was the only new one Dad bought, though near the end of his life he wanted a new Datsun pickup. He wasn't selfish and didn't begrudge my use of the car to visit Inamorata, a misty intellect he admired, but if I was at the wheel he kept pressing imaginary brakes on his side to slow me. My only incident with the car was on a night when Inamorata and I went on a drive, rather than sitting at her kitchen table and talking or watching TV in the living room, with her mother in attendance, and as I swung into a curve through a grove of trees she cried, "What's that!" and at her cry I saw a deer on my side, a huge antlered stag, leap high. He cleared the hood before my foot got near the brake and we heard his rear hooves clack against the windshield. Not a pit or crack in the glass. Not a scratch on the car. The deer went off into the trees in brush-walloping leaps.

Another time, Dad and I were on a summer trip to Wisconsin, carrying on the car top (lashed down with ropes) a long carton that contained a metal shower stall—the stand-alone type common at the time. He planned to install it as a backup in the basement of our uncle's farmhouse, and drove straight through the night, as he often did, but this time, toward the end, he started nodding off and asked me to take the wheel.

I came over a rise and recognized the buildings of our uncle's farm in the valley below, and stepped on the gas just as we swooped into the valley. I heard a rumble of ropes and in the rearview mirror saw the boxed shower go sailing off like a kite and land in the ditch on our side.

You could say my subconscious had an attack, and in its pour past the bars of the future I felt a scourge like stripes across my triple sin: driving too fast, responsible for the lousy lashing of the carton, and besides that, when the cardboard kite took off in a cartwheel and Dad rose from sleep at the noise, I yelled "*Shit!*"

I wheeled the car in a wobbly reverse to the carton, arms quaking, including the one over his seat, near his neck, and have an image of the way he pushed himself from his door and squared his fists on his hips. "What the—" he began. "Why, look!"—he started down the ditch—"only that corner of the carton looks smashed, where it hit down. Come on!"

I think he forgot others needed forgiveness, blinded to the guilt they felt by the residence of death that was his lot, and I followed in silence at his side to the carton resting on a cushioning mass of alfalfa. He was right, and once we got the bulky package to the farm by shoving it in the back seat and letting it stick out the open door—not far to go—he only had to tap out a corner and touch it up with appliance enamel before he installed it.

He was a plumber who could work sheet metal, as when he installed our new furnace, one of his skills. He was good with a hawk and trowel, able to skim rough coat over ceilings all day, which you ought to try for eight hours. Try it for one.

He kept chipping away at our house and had so many tools he could be taken for a professional carpenter. Attached to the house was a double garage with high windows, and he built a bench in a corner where he stored the tools and tinkered, and when he worked part time on one of the family carpentry crews, overseen by his brothers, they gave him odd jobs.

"Don't let Everett have a hammer!" I heard one cry, after Dad drove the head of one through a one-by-twelve in his miss of a nail—his brothers amused by his carpentry skills. But if they were in town or the neighboring countryside and needed a tool, they came to our garage, to his workbench, and grabbed it, petty theft they indulged in so often Dad had to travel to worksites to repossess them, and often a brother would say, "Hey, Everett, what are you *doing?* That's my hammer!"

So he marked his tools by filing three aligned grooves into the hardest metal of each, and when he went on his rounds he showed whatever was in his hand and said, "No, this is my mark. See?" I think of this when I come across one of his books in my library, not with three grooves but the slanting perfection of his signature on an endpaper, often with a date below, in classics sold in sets in the 1930s and 1940s.

It's an odd season for a winter storm, after a December and January in the thirties and forties, sometimes fifties, with February up to sixty, but then a sudden seep from the thirties to below zero, breath unfurling in billows fit for the beard on Santa Claus, and then snow, a first evening of light snow, then snow every which way, powered finally by an east wind, leaving such a drench of humidity it clipped an ache to my outer ear, as I noted to our woodcutter, John.

He threw aside the carcass of a stump that caused his red-blond beard to crumple double over his chest, and said, "Oh, yeah, *that* feeling. Yup. I noticed it ice-fishing."

My ears generally aren't affected in our arid geography, the sky so saturated now it causes the air to absorb light and shine like rime. Once when I filled the furnace late at night, after twelve, I noticed from the picture window of the house how smoke rolled from its stack into the atmosphere like a long slow slug in a time-lapse movie taking a spinning exit from a rifle barrel, revolving in a smoking swirl that folded into a quilted cloud spreading to the breadth of a real cloud, as seen from inside, in a colloidal commotion of substance, and dragged itself over the window in a fume I stepped back from, as if the final round fired by the protagonist of my first novel over Lake Michigan, in the direction of the island of Manitou, a native name for God, was headed home. I went out the door and saw extensions of the smoking cloud climb the roof like groping fingers and arrange themselves in thicker bands that bent and arched as I followed them, stepping down the steps I've used a thousand times, and then wafted above the three-story tower you and I built in one of my designing crazes. There it had the appearance of a Milky Way, a three-quarter moon shining through it, as if the planes of our carpentry illustrated a celestial concept, the past and present parted by the prow of the future, the roof edge of the tower that will stand after I'm gone.

Once in the ditch beside me, in the midst of a snow like this, I came up fast on a golden eagle perched on bloody snow, and then saw the carcass of a deer beneath. The eagle cranked its bloody beak toward me, as if assessing whether it could take on a Bronco, wings wafting for a lift as it gave a blinking grim assessment, and then was off in a slow glide at a low height in a loop for its return to the deer.

Nothing is hidden. Nothing is buried beyond discovery. Everything will be revealed. So to conclude about the deer: when it slid up the highway from our impact, bumping into the ditch, and I got out on giving legs at the shriek of the radiator, I ran to the edge of the road before I got back in the car for my run home. The deer lay beneath the level of the car's headlights, unmoving, and a smaller deer, not a fawn but not a yearling either, appeared out of the darkness, bounding in leaps around its mother, and then was off into the dark again.

I am the offspring of a mother dead held by a *Dod*.

He was a careful driver, never in an accident, though he drove from coast to coast a dozen times, and when he traded in the car I called Dad's car for a slightly used one, it was to please his second wife. After she died, three years later, my sister Mary Lois, news bringer and family historian, called to say that in the space of a month Dad had sideswiped a car, sliding on ice, and rear-ended another. I called him and asked what was up, what was wrong, what was happening, and heard a rueful laugh.

"Oh, I don't know," he said. "Daydreaming, I guess."

Two years later I was in New York, waiting for *Beyond the Bedroom Wall* to come out, when he called and asked if I would meet him at JFK during a layover he had on a return flight from Rome. It was his first trip to Europe, which he took because his cancer was resistant to chemotherapy, as I feared, and as a last resort he wanted to gather with the pilgrims in St. Paul's and receive a blessing from the Pope. He asked me to meet him for an hour at JFK on the day of his layover. I barely got a cab in time, was sure I wouldn't make it, but once I got to the terminal I saw him walking toward me.

He glanced over my shoulder, shook my hand, and then glanced over my shoulder again, as if death were at my back and the sight of it was disheartening. "I thought Michael would be with you," he said.

"Michael?"

"Your editor. Didn't you say he wanted to meet me?"

"Oh, he wanted to be here," I said, inventing, because I had forgotten this, and had probably said on the phone that Michael would be at the airport with me. "Something came up."

"That's too bad."

I held up the *Times Book Review* with my picture and Gardner's review on its cover.

"You couldn't ask for better placement," he said. "Is it a good review?"

"Yes."

"May I have it?"

"I brought it for you."

"I always had faith in you, Larry, no matter what, and never gave up my prayers for you. I'm happy to be able to say that." He took me in an embrace and I bumped against the huge and lumpy protuberance of his fatal tumor.

The day of his funeral, one of his brothers walked up outside the parish hall, after a meal I couldn't eat, and put a hand on my shoulder. "I felt so sorry for your dad these last years," he said. "No matter where he went, when he was driving, he always got lost. He said he was coming to visit us and late one night the telephone rang. It was Everett. He was at the local police station. 'Louie,' he said, 'Louie, come and get me!' 'What on earth are you doing at the police station?' I asked. 'I'm lost!' he said. 'I got lost on my way to your place and I'm so lost I don't know where I am! The police brought me here. Come and get me.' I felt so bad when I saw him at the station, sitting on a bench, his head in his hands. 'My big brother's slipping,' I thought. He got up and embraced me and said, 'Oh, Louie, I'm so lost!'"

It was the first I'd heard of this, and I saw the shower stall sailing away and the hooves of the stag striking the windshield, and a moment I held at bay, when I was standing beside his grave next to the closed casket that held his body, swarmed over me, and I felt him heading in the direction language can define only as endlessness, eternity, to the silence of the hidden north, the primary direction he never lost sight of or lost in his pursuit of it, happy to give his last goodbye.

What he planned to do with the rest of his life, after he bought the Datsun pickup, was buy a piece of land on his friend's farm in North Dakota, the one he worked on every spring once school was out, until planting season was over.

"That's my goal," he said. "Just a few acres."

I have his favorite hawk and trowel, and at a long-ago auction I bought a wood toolbox the size of a steamer trunk, with a hinged cover, painted black, and last year stenciled the initials of his father, the original carpenter, with three given names, as you have, Joseph, on its lid, and intend to stencil E C W somewhere, when I find the right artifact. For now I have a few of his tools on the bench I hurry to every day over the summer, busy with another remodeling or repair project, as numerous as the stacks of writing in different stages in my office, the two often coinciding—a nook done the week a novel is. Over the summer as dusk thickens to dark at 10:00 in our northern hemisphere, I put away the tools, as I never used to do, and when my fingertips touch a triple line of grooves, the intercom in me sends up a single word, *Dad*.

Between our head-on with the pickup and the lion-like crush of the PTO, you come to the farm with Jen and Timothy and Valerie for Christmas, the memory of it so persistent it seems like the winter you're in the Bronco beside me. The week before you arrived, I was asked to tape a reading appropriate to the season by Prairie Public Radio. I decided on a passage from *Born Brothers*, when Charles wakes to carols being piped from the Hyatt church and goes to the living room to check on the gifts and feels so unworthy at the bounty he finds that he considers walking out into the cold, but his father appears in his robe and carries him back to bed.

Your mother got me to the studio in Bismarck minutes before the taping—I hate to be late—and said she would pick me up in half an hour. In the midst of the reading, my father rose from the pages and I had trouble going on, suspended in catches and hesitations as I tried to recover from the jolt of his presence. I believed the reading would settle the peace between us, his casket twenty-five years in the ground, but found my hope reversing as I struggled for breath and control of my voice, and finally did a sinking dive into the prose, so familiar I could alter sentences as I read, and at the end the emotion that overtook me was gone, my scattered interior gathered in the conclusion, and I left the studio and went up the steps of the station with a light-headed sense.

Care wasn't outside, so I went toward a distant service station for a reward, and as I came to a diner I swung wide of its parking lot to a broad sward beside a highway busier than the interstate, the state capitol tower two blocks away, and realized I was wearing running shoes, which I don't usually wear outside the house to minimize the appearance of a geezer, and saw the shoes plunge in a rubbery way into— *What?*

Grass, bright green, the *green* green of Lorca, an entire ditch of it bordering the highway all the way ahead to where it bent over a hill, an essence of grace across the season after the awful winter of 1997, and with caroling and a decorated tree and pine scent and colored lights from the passage suspended in memory,

I stepped into Christmas, the transforming moment of Charles and his father as unearthly as the green under my feet. I felt the heavy hardback I used for the taping gripped in one hand and found I was fumbling with the other for my glasses, the spongy case that held them, and discovered I'd zipped it into my jacket pocket, the glasses there, not sitting eyeless in the studio, as I feared.

I got a Coke and did my duty at the service station, or did that in reverse, and walked to the studio on its hill and found Care in the car, waiting. I got in and entered her penumbra as she fluffed at her hair in the driver's visor mirror, no word from her, no question, and felt a gallop of my heart at her assertion of equality—hair first, friend—and sensed the Christological content of our forty years of marriage, which reaches to you, Joseph, as to any parent's proud offspring, or pride in you as a son (I find I can't say this right, perhaps because I never told you or your sisters I was proud of you but avoided it in an effort to avoid pride), and on Christmas Eve we listen to my reading on the radio as we sit at dinner, you and Jen at the table, Timothy attentive, his wide-spaced brown eyes (an inheritance from his mother) the loveliest I've seen, the remains of our meal set aside, and hear the first note of my voice head south with emotion at the sight of the unexpected gifts, "I'm not ah ee o—" going out over the ether in an awful moment—"*worthy*"—a downward catch, and I picture my father the way I've pictured him these past months, pacing a room at an unreachable level, a realistic heaven, no jeweled fantasy overlaid with gold, *in another place*, a pipe gripped in his teeth, his steps picking up when I think of an unpaid bill, and realize the pacing isn't from duress but is the patient assurance of the amiable.

Not worthy of this.

I meant not worthy of him as a father, and in *Born Brothers*, after his death, I was able to extend my gratitude to him in the scene between father and son, when the son feels an animating wind entering his cells as if his father is his savior—face bronzed by an array of Christmas lights—wearing an Indian blanket bathrobe like the colorful covenant robe of Joseph.

I sat at his bedside the last weeks of his dying, after we were more than reconciled, but I still bore leaden buckets of guilt at how I judged him and handed not such admirable traits to fictional fathers, criticized his eating habits, his talk, gestures, the house I was mooching from him to live in, exiling him to the basement or to his office in an enclosed porch, where he took up the pacing I see him enacting now, hands in his pockets, or to the garage outside, where he sat and faced his potbellied stove aglow with burning wood scraps, like the stove he fired up for my mother when she taught in a country school, before they were married, where she learned to contend with the round-house of roughhousing carved by "the boys," as she called us, before her daughters arrived—Dad sitting in suspension at the glowing stove, unmoving for too long for a man of passion in his fifties, *unless he's starting to write a book*, as I've encouraged him to do, because I did do that, and would settle in a chair at the stove with him and sit silent, communing with his aura—the scene I chose to read an offering like the incense of wood-smoke for him—the recording our family at the table listens to now, and understand he and I are reconciled in a physical sense, too, in a way I never would have thought to disclose: *I and my father are one.*

At the catch in my voice, I'm suspended in the ether across the countryside, held in radio waves three hundred miles to Fargo, the source of the broadcast, and sit in silence under your eyes, Joseph, in a frozen stare of my own, wondering when I'll resume the story as the starved silence extends, and when at last I hear myself speak the next line, partly undone, I see your eyes glaze over with the emotion of a listener whose only thought is to be kind.

Timothy stares up at you with the adoration of a lover, moved by your emotion, his wide brown eyes registering his entry into your state. He will be fine.

So when we meet outside the illusions we contend with, let's begin beyond the bounds of any book, our feet planted in the future, absolved of every question from the past, and clasp each other in recognition of that (if I'm not in the house or my office, you'll find me in the fields where I receive my daily dose of eternity), while I reach back through twelve books to my first and find the final round go spiraling away from the rifle toward Manitou and follow the slug until it comes sailing over the sea-wash of grass spread across the plains in a breadth greater than any lake in the lower forty-eight, and like so many projectiles from the past headed into orbit but slowed by the existential declination of extended flight, I know that someday the centrifuge of earth will send me spinning off like it, as the PTO could have sent shreds of me flying abroad, and I know that the spirit of me will remain a part of the cloud of witnesses gathered that day at the tractor drawbar, infusing our former histories with sense, and I know, too, that at the end of the arc of the slug, on the final page of this book, I'll pluck it from the air, as I do, the heated and worn weight of it hardly more than a grain of wheat in my hand—seed destined to die in order to spring to life in another story.

C O D A

Or call it north to coda, to end a summer day, with clouds massed like the presence of that otherworld gathered at the PTO, but forecasters have warned of changes in IT, the weather here, I mean now—troubling thunderstorms for the afternoon. I have hay windrowed from a week ago, so I hurry to the Case 930, huge above the baler, with room on its platform for another person, so if my father and I are one, he's aboard.

I head in fifth to the field, an alfalfa strip invaded by brome. Spears of grass and alfalfa's curling stems pierce the dry-yellow windrow with shoots of green—rain and then days of a hundred-degree bake—the moisture retained a sign of profit to our planting on this hill. Rivers of green pour down the spaces between windrows. The teeth of the pick-up feed the hay in an unbroken blanket into the baler, the packer arm flexing like an

269

elbow in its hookup to the flywheel, driving the packer into the chamber in heart-shaking jolts.

My high seat sways and jolts like a mechanical barroom bull while I hold to the wheel to keep myself from free flight into the skull-crushing wallops, *ka-chung,* the error of a fall my last, as I know.

The only time I nearly lost my seat was on a tractor I bought in a field twenty miles away and in my hurry to get it back, flying along in the grass of a ditch in road gear, I didn't see a drainage culvert in time to remember I had to hit a hand clutch, and flew up with a force that might have made heaven if my hams hadn't hit the wheel so hard they went numb as my intestines leaped for my teeth.

Timothy, and *vetch,* and *clover,* the phrase repeats itself to the rhythm of the baler, as if I'm speaking it aloud—a variety of grasses I hope to plant to heal the hill further. Bales tied tight, green streaked, tumble onto the stubble, a satisfying sight—both knotters tying after I sharpened a knotting knife. Then a strew of loose hay over the green sward behind and I see at the front of the baler that a twine is absent, its spool used up. I meant to grab a pair of spools in my rush against the rain and now it's as if I've brought a built-in timer: *Quit,* it says, *Quit while you can.*

Because rain is arriving. Tentacles of lightning grip a butte to the west, the concussion so sudden through my trap-shooter earmuffs I jump. Drops sharp as sharpened pencils assault my arms and back. I jerk the lever to disengage the PTO, the baler's banging lessening as its packer slows, then hit neutral and hop off to raise the steel-fingered pick-up. A shaft of lightning with a wallop of thunder right after is loud enough to knock freckles off—eardrums quivering under the muffs in its aftershock, loosing an unvoiced, *Spare me!*—all life a step toward death under the lintel of heaven's gate, my father and others gathered close in the interim.

I climb back on and find fifth and by now I'm soaked, my work shirt a clinging blue skin, *baby blue*, as I head home along a row of honeysuckle we planted decades ago. With no child on the tractor, none on a hayrack, no children in the fields, their bright clothes a blare, I'm a hollow husk, and once in the house, where I shake off rain, dripping, Care comes up to me, no children at our waists or knees, tugging at our clothes, and takes me in her arms, and when my arms wrap around her I press my rib upon a loveliness most cherished in my world, those outer and inner spheres that interleave, past and future orbiting in quirky equilibrium with hers and the branches of our families, all those on the four sides, and though we hold the best of them in both our selves, we do not hold creation itself, as it may seem, but contain in our embrace the memory of my mother and father, her father and sister Val; Bill and Emmy and Candida and Roger and Lee Goerner and Chuck Shattuck and Tom McGrath, Oscar Rogers and the living, our remaining mother, June; Michael di Capua, Don Fehr and the people at Perseus, Counterpoint again a Shoemaker orb, Dr. George and Kathy, Dr. Rog and Jan, Jan Dennis, savior of the farm, Marty and Phyllis, Nobuya and Michiko, Rick Watson and Chuck Suchy and Shadd Piehl and Denise Lajimodiere; Roberta Green Ahmanson and Howard and Ann Dahl, sustainers; the gracious Lannan Foundation, epitomized by Martha Jessup, angel Carolyn Forché and Bill Edgar, with words in season, and Pam and Mark and Michael Beard and Ursula, Bill and Dina, Gary and Myra, Tom and DeAnne and Bill and Rollie and the flock at Lemmon, along with poet and trainer Keith; Ed and Sue and

Stephen and Wanda and Chris and Helen, Michael and Nick, Randy and Ann, and last and so first, our children, Newlyn and Ben, Joseph and Jen, Ruth and Jeremiah, parent queller Laurel, plus the line of grandchildren—Medora and Camilla and Christian and Rue and Judith, Timothy and Valerie, and Lane; honest brother Dan, tall and handsome Chuck, Mary Lois the historian, Marce the prophetess, and their husbands and wives and children and grandchildren, too, along with those who bother to write, whether I answer or not, and colleagues and friends and students so numerous it would take a pulped tree to list them—all these and more are present in our embrace, their presence preserved in us as long as our memories persevere in their entwined state, so *Thank You.*

Thank you, Care, and *thank you all.*